REVEALED

Hope in the Vision of the Future

Werner Kniesel

Foreword by Larry Stockstill

Printed in Canada.

Word Alive Press
131 Cordite Road, Winnipeg, Manitoba, R3W 1S1
www.wordalivepress.ca

MIX
Paper from
responsible sources
FSC® C016245

Library and Archives Canada Cataloguing in Publication

Kniesel, Werner, 1938-
    Revealed : hope in the vision of the future / Werner
Kniesel ; foreword by Larry Stockstill.

ISBN 978-1-77069-355-5

    1. Bible. N.T. Revelation--Criticism, interpretation, etc.
I. Title.

BS2825.52.K58 2011   228'.06   C2011-906745-5

CONTENTS

FOREWORD

The world seems to be falling apart! Is this something to fear, or an anticipation of a new world Jesus is establishing?

For many years, Pastor Werner Kniesel and I have developed a mutual friendship and camaraderie in church planting. He has pastored one of the largest churches in Europe in Zurich, Switzerland. His marriage and life character are impeccable. His reputation with world leaders is renowned. His greatest quality, however, is his *humility*. Every moment I have spent with Werner over the years has left me more hungry to be like Jesus!

This volume on Revelation comes from many years of purity in ministry, a pastoral heart for people, and focus on the salvation of the lost. In this timely treatise, Pastor Werner, "boils it all down" to that theme as the most important activity of the church. Though the book intricately explains all the seals, trumpets, and bowls of the Revelation, it maintains the focus upon Jesus and His desire to rescue men and women from the lake of fire.

This is not a book to simply *broaden* your knowledge. It is written from the heart of a "soul winner" with hopes that you will take this work as a personal mandate to rescue the lost. Read it, digest it, then distribute it to friends, neighbors and family who are not ready for eternity. When all the books are written and destroyed by the brightness of His coming, only those that were used to deliver people from the lake of fire will be rewarded!

Congratulations on discovering this simple, yet profound, manual on the Revelation. I have spent six months teaching it to our church and they have been immensely blessed. Congratulations, Werner, on completing a life work on your most important message to reach the lost. May the Kingdom of God expand exponentially through every printed copy. Keep your eyes on the skies and your "hand to the plow." *You* are a part of the final harvest of souls, and it is beginning *now!*

Larry Stockstill

ACKNOWLEGEMENTS

My appreciation goes to:

My dear wife Hedi, who so faithfully has been at my side ministering with me during so many years.

The staff and congregation of CZB Zurich with whom I had the privilege to share twenty-four years.

Trudy Rittmeyer, my sister, who translated the German manuscript into English.

The staff of Word Alive Press for their professional cooperation at all levels.

Larry Stockstill, a dear Pastor and friend who loves the Lord, the church and its mission, for his example and inspiration to me.

Most of all, to Jesus my Lord and the wonderful Helper He gave, the Holy Spirit, for what they mean to me and my ministry.

INTRODUCTION TO REVELATION

As a Christian, one should read and study the book of Revelation. For many, this book remains mysterious, but this should not be the case. Jesus said, *"Do not seal up the words of the prophecy of this book"* (Revelation 22:10). The Word of God promises blessings for both reader and student of this book.

As you read, you will soon be aware that much of Revelation is symbolic and will not be easily understood. The meaning of a passage can often be determined in relationship to the actual context, or in reference to the Old Testament. Jesus Himself explains the symbols that were revealed to John in the first chapter.

Revelation is not a book of disorder or confusion. I believe that we find two accounts of similar events. The first one of these accounts starts with Revelation 4 and continues to the end of Revelation 11. It says, in Revelation 10:7, *"But in the days when the seventh angel is about to sound his trumpet, the mystery of God will be accomplished, just as he announced to his servants the prophets."*

The second account begins with Revelation 12. The same events are portrayed, but these last chapters give us more insight and enlightenment. I would like to point out that much of what God says and does is confirmed by two or three witnesses. When Pharaoh had his dreams concerning the future of Egypt, he did not just have one dream, but two different dreams with identical meanings. We can find the same principle at work in Daniel, to whom the future kingdoms of the world were revealed. He had one vision in Daniel 2, and another in Daniel 7. The two passages revealed the same truth in order to make the message more understandable and complete. In Revelation, God gave John a first vision, and then a second one. Both visions complement each other and produce a clearer picture. We shall study the Book of Revelation accordingly.

There are many different opinions concerning the interpretation of this book. There is agreement as to the main features, but not always to the details found in the writings. There are actually two interpretive theories. The first bases everything on history, the Historist Interpretation, which views Revelation 4–19 as the Dispensation of the Church. Everything written in these chapters is explained in view of the last two thousand years of history. The other theory is the Futurist Interpretation, which states that Chapters 1–3 pertain directly to the Church, while the remaining chapters are a description of the End Times.

We shall be discussing the Futurist Interpretation not simply out of curiosity, but because we live in the closing times of the Church. We should know about some of the things that will happen to our Earth and to the people living on it. These truths should lead us to a deeper relationship with God and to an intentional effort to work for Him.

What is the actual relationship of the book of Revelation to the rest of the Bible? The gospel of Jesus Christ is the basis of Revelation. Right at the beginning of the first chapter, John points to the Gospel. These opening passages speak of Jesus as the Son of God. They also state that Jesus was born and resurrected. This is the basis of the Gospel of Salvation. The Son of God came, died, and rose again. John also states that salvation is only possible through Jesus Christ, then goes on to show the result of faith for those who accept this salvation, have direct access to God the Father, and have become priests. The first chapter shows us that Jesus has the power over Death and Hell. We are also told that Jesus will return and that there will be a judgment over the people who have rejected Christ. The book of Revelation is in complete harmony and agreement with the preaching of the Apostles and the Prophets.

John's Vision of Christ

Following these introductory passages, we shall look into John's vision, which he describes in Revelation 1:9–20.

> *"I, John, your brother and companion in the suffering and kingdom and patient endurance that are ours in Jesus, was on the island of Patmos because of the word of God and the testimony of Jesus. On the Lord's Day I was in the Spirit, and I heard behind me a loud voice like a trumpet, which said: 'Write on a scroll what you see and send it to the seven churches: to Ephesus, Smyrna, Pergamum, Thyatira, Sardis, Philadelphia and Laodicea.' I turned round to see the voice that was speaking to me. And when I turned I saw seven golden lampstands, and among the lampstands was someone 'like a son of man', dressed in a robe reaching down to his feet and with a golden sash round his chest. His head and hair were white like wool, as white as snow, and his eyes were like blazing fire. His feet were like bronze glowing in a furnace, and his voice was like the sound of rushing waters. In his right hand he held seven stars, and out of his mouth came a sharp double-edged sword. His face was like the sun shining in all its brilliance. When I saw him, I fell at his feet as though dead. Then he placed his right hand on me and said: 'Do not be afraid. I am the First and the Last. I am the Living One; I was dead, and behold I am alive for ever and ever! And I hold the keys of death and Hades. Write, therefore, what you have seen, what is now and what will take place later. The mystery of the seven stars that you saw in my right hand and of the seven golden lampstands is this: The seven stars are the angels of the seven churches, and the seven lampstands are the seven churches.'"*

This took place around 96 A.D. All of the other Apostles were dead and the destruction of Jerusalem had occurred approximately twenty-five years earlier. There was a new generation of believers working in the churches. They were not primarily those who had accepted salvation at, or shortly after, Pentecost.

During this time, Jesus revealed Himself to one of His disciples, one of the three who had been closest to Him. If anyone knew Jesus well, it was John. Now, he saw Jesus in His present position and authority, not as He had been on earth—a human, demoted and humbled—but as the exalted King! Notice how he describes Him:

> "...dressed in a robe reaching down to his feet and with a golden sash round his chest. His head and hair were white like wool, as white as snow, and his eyes were like blazing fire. His feet were like bronze glowing in a furnace, and his voice was like the sound of rushing waters. In his right hand he held seven stars, and out of his mouth came a sharp double-edged sword. His face was like the sun shining in all its brilliance" (Revelation 1:14–16).

Can we picture and understand the Majesty of Jesus? Jesus Christ is the exalted King and Lord. He is holy. If John fell down as if dead, how will a sinner react when he stands before our Lord?

As Christians, we should never lose our faith in God because we have access to Him through the blood of Jesus. But, we should also never lose sight of the holiness of God's Majesty! With what kind of attitude do we go into the presence of God? Is it with reverence, respect and worship? John saw Him in the midst of the churches—then and now.

I have noticed that Jesus did not just address one individual in charge of all the churches; He addressed each church and each of its leaders individually. According to the Bible, in this vision a star represents the leader of a church. This vision shows us that Jesus is holding the stars in His right hand. When John saw all of this, he fell as though dead to the ground. Jesus touched him and said, *"Do not be afraid"* (Revelation 1:17). Then he told John to pay attention to the message. John was instructed to write what he saw, that which occurred ninety-six years after Christ, and that which would happen later. Most Bible teachers agree that these letters to the seven existing churches have a universal significance. They have a direct message, not only for the seven churches, but also for all Christendom throughout every generation. At that time, there were more than seven churches in Asia Minor. As far as we know, there were over one hundred churches, but only seven are mentioned. Did Jesus not care about the others? Of course He did. We read at the end of each letter, "He who has an ear, let him hear what the Spirit says to the churches." I believe that we can and must examine our church and our personal life according to the truths presented to these seven churches. There is no other place in the Bible that discusses the situation of a church in such a clear, understandable and vivid way as here. We cannot ignore this. We must pay attention.

These messages also portray the actual development of Christianity starting with the church in Ephesus, in the time of the apostles, right up to the church in Laodicea, which represents the lukewarm church of the end time.

We can see that Jesus appears to John as one who walks among His churches and judges and tests His churches in every aspect. He also keeps the leaders of the churches in His hand, and demands accountability from them. Just as Jesus showed that He held the stars in His hand, and that He demanded accountability from them, so He wants to show us that the moment will come when each Christian must give an account before Him. That is why He instructed the churches to rectify certain things, repent, and to change their minds.

I am certain that it will be an interesting journey as we travel through The Book of Revelation. We will discover how wonderful God's plan is for the church, for the nation of Israel, and for all people. We shall also learn how each person should heed His call as long as there is a time of grace.

The Letters

In my opinion, most Christians and pastors do not give the letters to the seven churches enough attention. Due to the leading and anointing of the Holy Spirit, the apostles and the early Christians were able to start many churches. Acts and the Epistles give us insight into the growth of some of these churches. Now, after some decades of existence, the Lord of the churches, Jesus, addressed them. I find this very noteworthy. These seven churches were selected to demonstrate the dangers and the wrong development that each Christian and each church will likely encounter throughout time. It is most important that we view these seven letters as a complete message to us from God. Jesus is the same yesterday, today and forever! What He states in these letters is for each person at all times. It is not necessary for Him to repeat things. He spoke. We must listen and obey.

John, who was often called Jesus' favorite disciple, received these messages under the influence of the vision he describes in Revelation 1:13-16. This overwhelming experience caused John to fall to the ground as if dead. After Jesus revived him, he received these messages for the seven churches. We can imagine what this meant to John. This was not a friendly little reminder, but a strong message of how God viewed the existing churches, and how He wants all churches to be throughout all times.

DO NOT LOSE THE MOST IMPORTANT

"To the angel of the church in Ephesus write: These are the words of him who holds the seven stars in his right hand and walks among the seven golden lampstands: I know your deeds, your hard work and your perseverance. I know that you cannot tolerate wicked men, that you have tested those who claim to be apostles but are not, and have found them false. You have persevered and have endured hardships for my name, and have not grown weary. Yet I hold this against you: You have forsaken your first love. Remember the height from which you have fallen! Repent and do the things you did at first. If you do not repent, I will come to you and remove your lampstand from its place. But you have this in your favor: You hate the practices of the Nicolaitans, which I also hate. He who has an ear, let him hear what the Spirit says to the churches. To him who overcomes, I will give the right to eat from the tree of life, which is in the paradise of God."

The church in Ephesus existed over nineteen hundred and forty years ago. It was a church where both young and old people followed and served God. Many people came to the Lord through this church, and they regularly met for services and fellowship in their homes.

Ephesus was the provincial capital and an important commercial center. It was home to the governor, and renowned as an influential, international seaport, the hub for three trade routes leading to Asia Minor. The Temple of Diana was in Ephesus. For that time, it was a very large structure, one hundred and thirty meters long and eighteen-and-a-half meters high. It stood on one hundred and twenty-seven marble pillars. Each had been a gift to the city. The whole community worked together to build this famous temple to Diana. People worshiping this goddess became hysterical and went into trances. Inside the temple were many small cubicles, and these were used to commit horrible sexual offences in honor of Diana. Today, Ephesus has almost been eradicated, and one can find little trace of the temple.

The church in Ephesus was started around 55 A.D. Eight years later, the letter to the Ephesians was written and sent to this growing church. The church had had a great beginning, which we can read about in Acts 19. The Word of God informs us that the first members of this church had experienced a thorough salvation and had been baptized in water, as Jesus had taught (Mark 16:16), The believers were filled with the Holy Spirit, and at the beginning accepted the Word of God with joy. Acts 19:11–12 reports extraordinary miracles, which the Lord performed through Paul's ministry. Even when Paul's handkerchiefs or belts were placed on the sick, illnesses vanished and evil spirits were driven out. This city experienced a wonderful visitation from God, and God responded in an unusual manner. The faith of these people was based on The Word of God and the evident demonstration of the power of the Holy Spirit.

The Bible tells of a day when books of magic and sorcery, objects concerned with the occult and ungodly items worth fifty-thousand silver coins, were burned publicly. These people understood what Jesus' message meant, what it entailed and what was required of them. They completely gave themselves to Jesus. In his farewell speech to the elders, Paul told them that he had taught them the complete ways of the Lord and that he had kept nothing from them. As we read Ephesians, we get the impression that we are reading about a wonderful, growing church, where the Apostle Paul was able to share his innermost knowledge about God's concept of a church. It was a lovely, fruitful church that brought honor and joy to the Lord.

Now we are coming to a later time, approximately forty years after this church was established, and around thirty-three years after receiving Paul's letter. As we read about what Jesus observed about this church, we learn that even though there was a completely new generation in the church, everything seemed the same. As far as outward appearances went, nothing had changed. They had learned that they should work for the Lord with great intensity and accomplishments. The people persevered, were patient and were taught that anything evil was not to be accepted in the church. All of this was observed. The church maintained the ability to differentiate between genuine and false workers in God's kingdom. The church had definite standards for those who were allowed to work in it. The church was prepared to be misunderstood in society for the sake of Jesus. Jesus said that this was good, and yet He found an enormous difference from forty or thirty-three years prior. Here we see that believing and well-meaning people, who desire to follow Jesus, can actually miss the real truth if they are lacking the revelation of Jesus Christ. In a space of forty years, the actual desires had been lost. Jesus saw this, and He had to reprimand them: *"You have forsaken your first love."* It is possible to hate what Jesus hates without loving what He loves. One more deduction is very evident in this case: it is possible to loathe false teachings and injustice and yet be spiritually insensitive and dead.

The revelation by Jesus was necessary to expose the true condition of the church. Jesus pointed out that the Ephesians had lost what was most important. What did Paul say in 1 Corinthians 13? When there is no love, good works are of no value to us. When there is no love, godliness is no longer what it should be. Love is not shown primarily by our works, through our efforts or our activity! Love is seen primarily in our relationship to God, to Jesus as our Lord and in our relationships to each other—to your wife, husband, parents, siblings and your brothers and sisters in the church.

Do we still have our first love for the Lord? How can I describe this? This is difficult to explain, but I would like to remind you how you felt when you realized that you were born again and your sins were forgiven. What was your main objective, then? Was it not that, above everything else, you wanted to please Jesus? You discussed everything with Jesus. He was so close to you that under no circumstance did you want to disappoint or hurt Him. When you went to church and, through the message, heard what God wanted you to do, you did it. You wanted to please the Lord. You were driven by that first love. As you began to serve in the church, you did it because you knew that this was the will of the Lord. Even though it took time and energy, you did it gladly, because you were on fire for Jesus.

Notice what Jesus is saying. He does not say we should give up our activities for Him, but He questions whether they originate out of genuine love. Our love for Jesus has certain characteristics: it is evident in our desire to be close to Him. It is apparent in our desire to serve Him, not just to work for Him—there is a difference. This is noticeable when two people are in love. They are captivated with each other, and as long as this feeling continues, everything goes well. They desire to be close to one another, and look for any reason to be together. They love to do things for each other, and regardless of obstacles find a way to do them.

Do we still have this love for our Lord Jesus? If it is not there anymore, we have lost what is most important. This is exactly what Jesus is saying here, what the Ephesians had lost. In spite of this, Ephesus still appeared to be a beautiful, exemplary church, which impressed many people. But Jesus said something else about this church when He called out, *"Repent."*

Who called this out? It was the One who held the stars in His hand and who walks in the midst of the church. To whom was this call directed? The Bible says, *"To the angel of the church in Ephesus."* Jesus did not tell the angel to call a church meeting to see whether it would be a good time to repent; He ordered him to repent. It is good for us to pay attention to the things our Lord deems most important, and it is absolutely possible to lose sight of them.

Jesus wants us to think about how it was at the beginning of our journey of faith, and to repent. If there is no repentance, then the lampstand will be pushed out of its position. The lampstands represent the churches. What does Jesus mean? If this church did not repent, then it would soon not exist. Jesus speaks directly to each person and says, *"He who has an ear, let him hear."* This is very personal. The call to repent and to change has to occur in each individual—in me, in you, in each of us. The call also goes out not just to the Ephesians, but to all churches, *"Let him hear what the Spirit says to the churches!"* At this time, the Ephesians did not know they would soon be facing persecution of the Christians, and then they would have to be reminded of this statement.

God is eager to direct His church to the right path. He speaks to us for our own good. The Lord does not want us to deceive ourselves. He would prefer that one day we would stand before Him, to be with Him, and that God's blessings would remain on us. Our time on earth is short and passes quickly. The Bible says it is like a vapor. God wants to help us recognize that He has a wonderful plan for His people and for His children. When we depart from this plan, He comes to us with His goodness and mercy, reprimands us, and shakes us up. He wants us to reach the goal He has set before us, and to be that for which He has called us.

ARE YOU FAITHFUL?

"To the angel of the church in Smyrna write: These are the words of him who is the First and the Last, who died and came to life again. I know your afflictions and your poverty —yet you are rich! I know the slander of those who say they are Jews and are not, but are a synagogue of Satan. Do not be afraid of what you are about to suffer. I tell you, the devil will put some of you in prison to test you, and you will suffer persecution for ten days. Be faithful, even to the point of death, and I will give you the crown of life. He who has an ear, let him hear what the Spirit says to the churches. He who overcomes will not be hurt at all by the second death."

Smyrna is situated about fifty-five kilometers north of the large seaport, Ephesus. Smyrna surprisingly had quite a good road system, which was not the norm of the day. There were a number of temples in Smyrna, and it had a reputation as perhaps the most modern and most beautiful city of that time. However, there was one big problem. When the city was planned, they forgot to build in a sewer system. As a result, the city streets were flooded every time it rained, and even though it was a beautiful city, this problem gave it a horrible reputation.

Smyrna was an important political city. The population was pro-Roman; this was noticed by Caesar. The Roman Empire consisted of many nations, cities, races and religions, and this made it difficult to unify. The military was able to put pressure on a nation for a limited time. As soon as military rule was relaxed, it became difficult keep the conquered lands unified within the empire. It was decided that the way to do this was to capitalize on the religious feelings of the people from various races and nations. As a result, the Caesar Cult was born, and Caesar was worshipped as god. A similar event happened under Nebuchadnezzar. He tried to unify people by forcing all of them to bow down and worship only his statue. King Darius did the same thing. He erected a picture and gave the decree that for thirty days, only that picture could be worshipped. Politicians used the people's need for religion for their purposes.

Today Smyrna is called Izmir, with a population of approximately two hundred and fifty thousand. This city had been destroyed several times but was always rebuilt. The church in Smyrna received a letter from John, who told them that the Lord had revealed Himself to him. They knew John, and they knew he would never have dared to say something like this if it had not happened. Do we require such a letter from God? Actually, we have one. This letter not only exposes the character of the church in Smyrna, but it shows what can occur at any time in a church of Jesus. That is why each of these admonitions ends with, *"He who has an ear, let him hear what the Spirit says."* Jesus introduces Himself as, *"him who is the First and the Last, who died and came to life again."*

The people of Smyrna worshipped Dionysius, the god of fertility. They claimed that at one time Dionysius had been dead but he had come back to life, and that is why he was now able to bring about fertility. However, Jesus said, *"I was dead and came back to life, I am the first and the last, I am Lord of all, I am the only God."*

The introduction of the Caesar Cult caused a persecution for the church. All Roman citizens, including the people in Smyrna, were expected to offer incense on an altar at least once a year, in honor of Caesar. This was strictly controlled through registration, and each one who did it received a certificate or a stamp. Besides this, people were allowed to follow the religion of their choice, but this Law had to be obeyed. We can imagine the inner turmoil facing the Christians. They refused to obey this Law, and were known as lawbreakers. This resulted in persecution.

How was it in the time of Daniel? There was a decree Daniel could not keep, and thus he was convicted as a lawbreaker. Can we recognize the tricks of the devil? At the time John received this message, it was likely that Polycarp was the Bishop and Leader of the church in Smyrna. Polycarp was taken prisoner during one of the heathen festivals. The people yelled, "Let us capture Polycarp so that he can now bring Caesar an offering." They gave him the chance to do so. However, he said, as quoted from the History of the Church, "I have served Christ for eighty-six years; He has never deserted me. How can I blaspheme my King, the one who has saved me?" On that very day, he was burned alive. From the flames his voice could be heard as he prayed, "I thank you, Father, that you have considered me worthy to experience this day and this hour, to become a martyr and to have a part in the suffering of Jesus."

The antichrist will enforce a similar system. You can believe whatever you want, but if you will not adhere to his sovereign authority, and will not accept his sign on your forehead or on your right hand, persecution will follow.

Jesus says, *"Do not be afraid of what you will have to undergo. Be faithful until death."* By this He does not mean that we should be faithful until we die. It says be faithful, even if it causes your death—faithful unto death. What, exactly, is faithfulness? It is an inner attitude, a total commitment, which is closely related to truth. Your yes is a yes and your no a no. Jesus said we should be faithful. Have you ever asked yourself whether you are faithful?

In our time, faithfulness has lost its value. Faithfulness in marriage is hardly ever discussed. Tolerance is the accepted attitude of today. Jesus, however, looks for faithfulness. We should be faithful to God and to the church, and faithful to the promises made to the Lord.

Jesus wants us to know that if we want to reach the goal to be part of the Rapture, we must not lose our first love, and we must practice faithfulness.

Can God not prevent persecution? Can He not protect His children? In 2 Corinthians we read about all of the persecutions that Paul went through. Jesus had said that His followers will experience persecutions.

What exactly are persecutions and the things the Bible speaks of, such as experiencing slander and being thrown into prison? We call it persecution, but what is it really? Persecution is always started by the devil. According to the devil, persecution is meant to ruin one's faith. God allows persecution so that we can prove our faith. That is the difference. The devil wants to quench the fire; Jesus wants to turn it into a blaze.

It is possible that we will experience things in our personal life that others do not. There are things in our life that have not been sent by God, but have been allowed by Him so that we can prove our Christianity. Don't think that God is unfair; think of it as a refining and preparation process by God. Persecution does not destroy the Church. It actually seems that God allows persecution to come when the spiritual life of a church becomes shallow, in order to wake up the Christians. God, in His Word, called out to the church in Smyrna and beyond that to all of us, *"Be faithful until death."*

I am certain that even in our western world, some Christians are being persecuted in their own homes, by their own families, simply because they are a Christian. Some are persecuted at their workplace, in schools and in neighborhoods. We all know how the media ridicule and belittle true, Bible-believing, Christians. We, however, should become more faithful to Christ in our desire to serve Him. We should always remember that He sees everything, He who is the First and the Last.

LIVING IN THE MIDST OF GREAT UNBELIEF

Revelation 2:12–17

> "To the angel of the church in Pergamum write: These are the words of him who has the sharp, double-edged sword. I know where you live—where Satan has his throne. Yet you remain true to my name. You did not renounce your faith in me, even in the days of Antipas, my faithful witness, who was put to death in your city—where Satan lives. Nevertheless, I have a few things against you: You have people there who hold to the teaching of Balaam, who taught Balak to entice the Israelites to sin by eating food sacrificed to idols and by committing sexual immorality. Likewise you also have those who hold to the teaching of the Nicolaitans. Repent therefore! Otherwise, I will soon come to you and will fight against them with the sword of my mouth. He who has an ear let him hear what the Spirit says to the churches. To him who overcomes, I will give some of the hidden manna. I will also give him a white stone with a new name written on it, known only to him who receives it."

What would our reaction be if this were addressed to the church in New York, London, or Toronto instead of Pergamum? We may find this amusing, but would this be so impossible? Is Christ not still the Lord of the church, who walks among His people, who holds the angels in His hand? We would certainly react differently if we would suddenly see our name here!

Jesus introduces Himself to this church as the one who has the sharp, double-edged sword. This is repeated in verse 16. In the Bible, the double-edged sword is referred to as the Word of God. Hebrews 4:12 says, *"For the word of God is living and active, sharper than any double-edged sword."* In the letter to the Ephesians, 6:17, it says, *"Take the helmet of salvation and the sword of the Spirit, which is the word of God."* Isaiah 11:3b–4 states:

> *"He will not judge by what he sees with his eyes, or decide by what he hears with his ears; but with righteousness he will judge the needy, with justice he will give decisions for the poor of the earth. He will strike the earth with the rod of his mouth; with the breath of his lips he will slay the wicked."*

It is evident that the people in the church in Pergamum no longer took the Word of God seriously. That is why the Lord introduced Himself as the author of the Word of God, and as the One who uses the Word of God, when necessary, to discipline them. It is obvious that there were people in Pergamum who were of the opinion that it was not necessary to completely accept the Word as they had received it.

Pergamum was a very interesting city. It was the capital and the educational center of the province, Asia Minor. Today we would call it a university city. Pergamum had a library with two hundred thousand books. This was the second-largest library of that time. We can well imagine the enormity of such an achievement, since printing had not yet been invented and each book had to be copied by hand. Parchment paper originated there. We notice the dependence on human wisdom and education. So it is no wonder that some people from the church valued philosophical views and education more than the Word of God.

The temple of Aesculapius, the god of healing, was in Pergamum. The people believed in supernatural healing and thus built a temple for this purpose. The symbol for this god of healing was a snake. Non-poisonous snakes were set free in the temple during the night. The people were encouraged to spend nights in the temple, and to allow these snakes to crawl over them. It was believed that these snakes were agents, directly sent by this idol, and therefore would bring about healing. The symbol of the snake has its origin in Pergamum. It has been accepted by the UN, has been put on stamps, appeared in pharmacies, and today is the medical symbol accepted by most of the world.

The Caesar Cult was very popular in Pergamum. We know that it was introduced for political reasons, and since Pergamum was a capital city, it is understandable that Caesar would be very eager to have his special cult there. As we have already stated, each citizen in the Roman Empire had to bring Caesar a yearly offering of incense. The Christians in Pergamum, as in other places, were in great danger whenever it was time to perform this ceremony. We can only speculate what *"where Satan has his throne"* means. There are several possibilities. Jesus mentioned it twice: *"where Satan lives, and where Satan has his throne."* It could be a reference to the temple and the throne of Aesculapius and the snakes. The snake is a picture of Satan for God's children. It could also be a reference to the worship of Caesar, which was very prevalent in that city, or it could refer to both.

Jesus also said that He knew what happened when Antipas, His faithful witness, was put to death. We do not know who Antipas was. It is said that at an opportune moment he was captured and persuaded in no uncertain terms to denounce his God. He refused to do so, and then was asked to at least go along with the majority. The opinion in that city was that the majority is always right. Antipas is said to have answered, "Even if I am the only one who believes in Jesus, I will remain faithful." Upon this, he was impaled on a brass pole and burned. Jesus did not forget him. Even if no one knows what you have suffered, and if no one knows what Christians in some countries are suffering today, Jesus knows.

He knew the church of Smyrna, and He had to admonish it. He said that He had a few things against them. There were people there who held to the teaching of Balaam, and those who held to the teaching of the Nicolaitans.

Balaam was a prophet who was supposed to curse Israel, but could not do so. God had called him and had anointed him for prophetic ministry. Whenever he was supposed to curse Israel, he blessed it. The king who had called him and ordered him to curse Israel was very angry.

Balaam had a weakness. He lived according to his human desires. He did not strive to totally please God. He was used by God, and his ministry and anointing were genuine, but for Balaam it was not problematic to separate his calling and his private life. When I am ministering, I should be open to God's leading. However, in moments when I am not ministering, my old nature can still take control. I have noticed that there are many Balaams around.

Balaam advised the king to mislead Israel and to get them to disobey God. God would then remove His protection and the king could capture them. The Holy Spirit tells us that there were some people in Pergamum who said it didn't really matter whether you lived a holy private life, as long as you fulfilled your ministry properly. Holiness had lost its importance to these people. As I look around, I can see that the devil is taking great pains to have us accept this attitude so that we will say it doesn't really matter how holy my life is, because God is so merciful. Do you recognize these thoughts? It is one thing to worship God in church, but a completely different thing to honor God in our daily life. Many see God's grace only as a cover-up for their sins.. Grace is given so that we would overcome our desires by crucifying our old nature, in order to live holy lives. God does not demand perfection. But it is a different matter to knowingly and continuously live in sin and to think that God's grace will cover everything.

Others held on to the teaching of the Nicolaitans, whose understanding was that there is a ruling class in the church which is superior to the others and has special privileges from God. The Bible teaches us that everyone is a priest; that means each Christian has direct and personal access to God. There is only one mediator between God and us; in this respect we are all equal, regardless of our calling. The Nicolaitans said, "God put people into the church that have direct access to God, and if you want to get to God, then you can do so only through them." These people began to control the believers. Did this only occur in that time? Does it still exist today? Jesus says that He hates this attitude. Repent! All of us have only one mediator, and that is to personally come to God.

When we hear the personal cry for repentance in our life, we should change our attitude, our ways, and turn to God's way. It could also mean, and in this case it did, that the church should change its path and attitude.

The main lesson for this church and for us is: without holiness, no one will see God.

BEWARE—
FALSE PROPHETS
DO EXIST!

REVELATION 2:18–29

"To the angel of the church in Thyatira write: These are the words of the Son of God, whose eyes are like blazing fire and whose feet are like burnished bronze. I know your deeds, your love and faith, your service and perseverance, and that you are now doing more than you did at first. Nevertheless, I have this against you: You tolerate that woman Jezebel, who calls herself a prophetess. By her teaching she misleads my servants into sexual immorality and the eating of food sacrificed to idols. I have given her time to repent of her immorality, but she is unwilling. So I will cast her on a bed of suffering, and I will make those who commit adultery with her suffer intensely, unless they repent of her ways. I will strike her children dead. Then all the churches will know that I am he who searches hearts and minds, and I will repay each of you according to your deeds. Now I say to the rest of you in Thyatira, to you who do not hold to her teaching and have not learned Satan's so-called deep secrets (I will not impose any other burden on you): Only hold on to what you have until I

come. To him who overcomes and does my will to the end, I will give authority over the nations— 'He will rule them with an iron scepter; he will dash them to pieces like pottery'—just as I have received authority from my Father. I will also give him the morning star. He who has an ear, let him hear what the Spirit says to the churches."

There is a definite pattern here. Jesus introduced himself to the churches. He pointed out the positive and admonished the negative. He always gave a promise to those who listen to Him and always finished with these words: *"He who has an ear, let him hear what the Spirit says to the churches."*

Thyatira was a city in the inner part of Asia Minor. Lydia, a dealer in purple cloth, who became a believer in the city of Philippi, came from this city. Compared to Pergamum, Smyrna or Ephesus, Thyatira was not an important political center. However, it was a famous economic and commercial city, especially in specific vocations and skilled trades. There were many guilds in this city, and history teaches that it was very difficult to make any commercial progress if one did not belong to a guild. The social meetings of these guilds consisted of heathen customs and immoral conduct. It was therefore difficult for Christians to live in this city and to carry on a business.

Thyatira had a temple dedicated to Apollo, the sun god, who was highly esteemed and worshipped in that city. The main medium of that temple was a woman called Sunbathe. We know that occult practices were carried on in the temple. She was the intermediary that supposedly spoke for the idol and delivered its instructions.

Jesus addresses this church by introducing Himself as *"the Son of God, whose eyes are like blazing fire and whose feet are like burnished bronze."* This is an interesting introduction! Jesus told them what He, the Son of God, had to say was important and relevant. He, the Lord, their God, had supreme authority. He wanted to let them know that everything, including the innermost thoughts of their hearts, was illuminated and completely known to Him. He knew them through and through; nothing could be hidden from Him. His eyes penetrate through everything. His feet, which were like burnished bronze, are a Biblical symbol of His authority to judge.

He knew all about them. He knew them thoroughly. He knew how they had increased their efforts to work for Him. Works that are accomplished through faith and love are good and genuine. It is amazing how Jesus praised the following positive traits: their faith, love, works and patience.

When we compare Ephesus and Thyatira, we can find only one difference. The Ephesians also had good works, faith, patience, and good sound doctrine, but they lacked the first love. We can see that the church in Thyatira had faith, patience, and good works, as well as that which Ephesus lacked, love. Yet they were reprimanded by Jesus because their teaching was incorrect.

Jesus told the Ephesians that if they did not repent and come back to the love they had at the beginning, He would remove their lampstand and they would not be able to be what they were supposed to be. He told the people in Thyatira that if they would not repent, He would strike them dead. It is obvious that Jesus places great importance on sound doctrine, which is essential to our Christian faith and life. The reprimand is found in verses 20–22:

> "Nevertheless, I have this against you: You tolerate that woman Jezebel, who calls herself a prophetess. By her teaching she misleads my servants into sexual immorality and the eating of food sacrificed to idols. I have given her time to repent of her immorality, but she is unwilling. So I will cast her on a bed of suffering, and I will make those who commit adultery with her suffer intensely, unless they repent of her ways."

We recognize the name Jezebel from the Old Testament. We read about her in 1 Kings. She was the wife of the godless king Ahab. The Bible tells us that she introduced idol worship to Israel in a cunning, pious manner. She did not decree that people had to denounce the true God. She managed to do this in a seductive way. When Ahab did not succeed in attaining Jezreel's vineyard, Jezebel came up with a plan. She proclaimed a great religious day of fasting. It is not wrong to fast, but this was a hypocritical fast in order to kill Jezreel. We are not certain whether the reference to Jezebel pertains to only one person or to a whole group.

What happened in Thyatira? The church was open to the gifts of the Spirit. They had accepted a prophetess who gave words of prophecy which led the believers to become unfaithful to God, and revert back to a carnal lifestyle. They no longer accepted the Word of God as the main authority for doctrine and guidelines. They gave more credence to so-called words of wisdom and prophetic messages. Is there anything wrong with gifts of the Spirit? Absolutely not! According to the Bible, these gifts were given to us for edification, comfort and admonition, but not to formulate a doctrine. Paul admonished Timothy with these words: *"Watch your life and doctrine closely"* (1 Timothy 4:16).

Doctrinal teaching may not be based on spiritual gifts, but only on the Word of God. The Bible tells us very clearly and distinctly that God will reject everything that does not agree with the word of God.

As I minister, I have noticed that during recent years there has been a tendency to increase such practices. Many people would rather listen to words of prophecy than to the Word of God. Their carnal nature is often supported through such words of prophecy.

In such churches or ministries, it is not uncommon to also find another issue that Jesus is addressing here: so-called deep secrets of Satan are known and taught—secrets about Satan not mentioned in the Bible. This fosters unbiblical teachings and practices. Holiness and living in the spirit are no longer the goals of the believers, but rather it is to have "new revelations!" The Bible teaches constantly that fear of God, the teachings of Jesus and obedience to the Word must be our foundation. These are, however, not popular concepts in our modern Christian world.

According to church history, this caused the development of the worship of icons, statues, saints and of Mary. These practices didn't just materialize by themselves; they were introduced through some kind of prophecy, when infallibility was bestowed upon the Pope. The Word of God was no longer the only source for doctrine.

Jesus gives this church and us the opportunity to repent. Isn't our Lord good? If we have allowed ourselves to be deceived, if we have sinned or gone astray, God calls us to repent, to ask Him for forgiveness, so that He can cleanse us and forgive us. Jesus said that unless they repent of their ways, judgment will come upon them.

COUNTERFEIT CHRISTIANITY

Revelation 3:1–6

"To the angel of the church in Sardis write: These are the words of him who holds the seven spirits of God and the seven stars. I know your deeds; you have a reputation of being alive, but you are dead. Wake up! Strengthen what remains and is about to die, for I have not found your deeds complete in the sight of my God. Remember therefore, what you have received and heard; obey it, and repent. But if you do not wake up, I will come like a thief, and you will not know at what time I will come to you. Yet you have a few people in Sardis who have not soiled their clothes. They will walk with me, dressed in white, for they are worthy. He who overcomes will, like them, be dressed in white. I will never blot out his name from the book of life, but will acknowledge his name before my Father and his angels. He who has an ear let him hear what the Spirit says to the churches."

According to today's standards, the cities of Ephesus, Smyrna, Pergamum, Thyatira, Sardis, Philadelphia and Laodicea were close in proximity to each other. Thyatira and Sardis were only about forty-five kilometers apart. This is insignificant for us, but in those days it was considered to be a great distance. Sardis was an important city because it was situated at the junction of busy highways and was more or less the axis between north-south and east-west traffic. Sardis was the first city to use coins, and money, as we know it, had its origin there. In 17 A.D., when Jesus was approximately twenty years old, Sardis was totally destroyed by an earthquake. Caesar Tiberius had the whole city rebuilt. He gave the citizens a five-year tax exemption so they could reconstruct their homes. At the time that John wrote this letter, Sardis was a relatively new city. There was very little idol worship there. It was a city known for entertainment and prosperity. The main interest of the citizens was to earn money through trade, and to have a good, pleasure-filled life.

Jesus had this written to the church in Sardis: *"You have a reputation of being alive, but you are dead."* Then he told them, *"Remember, therefore, what you received and heard: obey it, and repent."*

All of us who have heard the gospel and have been convicted and convinced that Jesus is Savior and Lord and realized that we were lost, put our trust in Jesus as Savior and accepted Him as our Lord. We were born again, and at the beginning we were very enthusiastic about Jesus and desired to please Him in everything we did. However, with many, this attitude slowly changed as time went by. Yes, we learned much from the Word of God, gained much knowledge, but we were not steadfast in the development of our spiritual life. Many have the idea that it is sufficient to have correct knowledge. Jesus tells us that we can increase in knowledge, but lose our spiritual life. The solution is to go back and remember how it really was when we accepted the truth about God. When someone recognizes that he needs the Savior and accepts Christ, he is like a child. In the presence of God he will break down and cry out for help. That is why Jesus says we should regain this attitude.

Jesus once told a very religious man, *"No one can see the kingdom of God, unless he is born again"* (John 3:3). It is not enough to know the proper teaching without having eternal life. We must be born again through repentance and having faith in the gospel.

I would like to glance at church history and at our present time. We have seen how the church in Thyatira, which tolerated the teachings of Jezebel, reflected a time when a so-called revelation could come into the church which did not correspond with the Word of God.

Accordingly, we learned from church history that the Gospel of Jesus was put into the background for several centuries. The Reformation came about due to some men God used. Much of the wrong teaching which had crept into the churches could only be rectified by paying attention to the Word of God. This resulted in Protestantism, which exists to this day.

The people were right to denounce the false teaching. They knew that one could only be saved through faith. They also knew that there was only one mediator between God and the people, and that is Jesus Christ, the Son of God. The Bible teaches that if we are a Christian, God recognizes us as a priest. They realized that God wants to build His church with all Christians in accordance with the influence of the Holy Spirit, Jesus' representative on Earth. They held to this knowledge and defended it. However, many of these people only accepted this teaching because it was reasonably correct. To this day, many people accept this opinion and defend it, but it is only a faith based on their intellect; there is no real life with God.

Why are so-called Evangelicals recognized within the Protestant churches? Many of them have realized that faith is not an intellectual matter, but it is a personal relationship with Jesus Christ. They understand that faith does not mean you have to comprehend everything, but you must have a living faith from God, which the Holy Spirit imparts through the new birth experience.

We can see why Jesus told that church, *"You have a reputation of being alive, but you are dead."* They did not accept the influence and work of the Holy Spirit in the new birth of a godly life, nor did they seek to be filled with the Spirit of God. This shows us how important it is to receive this new life from God and to be filled with the Holy Spirit, in order to live a godly life.

This church had a good doctrine, but lacked a Spirit-filled life. That is why Jesus had to tell them to wake up and "Remember therefore how you have received and heard; hold fast and repent." Does this not demonstrate a reversal? Jesus' words, *"Be watchful, and strengthen the things which remain, that are ready to die"* show us that there was something still alive. This church once had a godly life, but Jesus tells them to remember what they had received and what they had heard, and how it used to be. A childlike faith, a heart to please the father, living in the spirit, these things that were at the beginning, should be here now. He advised this church to remember what they had at the beginning, to turn back and to repent.

Jesus always recognizes what is genuine. He sees what is still alive among what has died. Is this not comforting? *"Yet you have a few people in Sardis who have not soiled their clothes. They will walk with me, dressed in white, for they are worthy."* He says that those who overcome will be clothed in white, and He will never blot out their names from the Book of Life, but He will acknowledge them before His Father and His angels.

A CHURCH
LOVED BY GOD

*"To the angel of the church in Philadelphia write: These are the
words of him who is holy and true, who holds the key of David.
What he opens no one can shut, and what he shuts no one can
open. I know your deeds. See, I have placed before you an open
door that no one can shut. I know that you have little strength,
yet you have kept my word and have not denied my name. I
will make those who are of the synagogue of Satan, who claim
to be Jews though they are not, but are liars—I will make them
come and fall down at your feet and acknowledge that I have
loved you. Since you have kept my command to endure
patiently, I will also keep you from the hour of trial that is going
to come upon the whole world to test those who live on the
earth. I am coming soon. Hold on to what you have, so that no
one will take your crown. Him who overcomes I will make a
pillar in the temple of my God. Never again will he leave it. I
will write on him the name of my God and the name of the city
of my God, the new Jerusalem, which is coming down out of
heaven from my God; and I will also write on him my new
name. He who has an ear let him hear what the Spirit says to
the churches."*

P hiladelphia was situated approximately forty-eight kilometers south of Sardis. Philadelphia was established around one hundred and eighty-nine years before the birth of Christ. It was around two hundred and seventy years old when John had his vision. This city did not grow just because people settled in the area. It was built with the definite aim to spread the Greek way of life, its ideals, culture, and language in Asia. Just like Sardis, Philadelphia was destroyed by an earthquake around 17 B.C. and was rebuilt by Caesar Tiberius. In order to thank Tiberius, the city fathers changed the name of the city, and for a time called it Neo-Caesarea. Later, it was reverted back to Philadelphia.

In the area around Philadelphia, vineyards were cultivated. Philadelphia had a large Jewish population. The city had the custom to honor a citizen who had accomplished something exceptional, or who rose to prominence in the city administration, by naming a pillar in one of the many temples after that person's name. Perhaps Jesus was thinking of this when He told them in the prophecy of their letter, *"Him who overcomes I will make a pillar in the temple of my God."*

Philadelphia was the last city to be conquered when the Muslims took over Asia Minor. It is interesting to note that the Christians in Philadelphia were the only ones who negotiated with the Muslims to be allowed to continue to ring their church bells. Islam had become so powerful in all the other cities that it was impossible to have any negotiations. Christianity was virtually eradicated.

It is encouraging that here, just as in the church of Smyrna, there was no admonition, *"I know your deeds."* God really does know everything. He not only knows what we do in our relationship with Him, He knows our whole life and our way of thinking. The Bible tells us that God notices everything. A prophet wrote in the Old Testament that God records everything in a special book.

God said that He gave them an open door, which He has opened for all people. Jesus Christ is the door to God for each individual, but a door is useless if you do not go through it. It is a reality that sin has built a wall between God and man. All people are sinners and lack the glory of God. This wall is real and no person, not even a Christian, is able to break it down. God gave us His Son as the way through this wall. We have to use it.

In church history, the church of Philadelphia refers to the same period of time as the church of Sardis in which Christianity mainly existed in name only, without evidence of a godly life. The church in Philadelphia was a mission-minded church with emphasis on outreach. Jesus encouraged this church, and realized what they had accomplished.

Church history tells us there was a time in which revivals broke out, and with them a missionary zeal in the churches was reborn. We may think our contributions to home and foreign missions are so minimal, but Jesus knows and sees what we are doing. Just as He notices our life, our business and actions, He really pays attention to what we do out of love for Him. On the day we stand before the throne of Jesus, many of us will ask, "Lord, when did I do that?" Jesus said that even if you just gave someone a cup of cold water, and you did it in His name, it will be credited to you. *"I have placed before you an open door."* He wants you to use it.

Jesus continued, saying, *"I know that you have little strength."* The little strength from God is strong enough to resist the devil, and to live a victorious life. Before Jesus left His disciples, He told them, *"You will receive power when the Holy Spirit comes on you"* (Acts 1:8). We do not have the same fullness of the Holy Spirit as Jesus did, but we do have a measure of the Spirit, sufficient for us, and therefore have power. Notice how important it is to be filled with the Holy Spirit!

God continues to say, *"You have kept my word."* This is the requirement— to be faithful to the Word of God. Jesus said, *"Heaven and earth will pass away, but my words will never pass away"* (Matthew 24:35). Regardless of what modern theology claims, the Word of God will remain just as He has said. The truths of the Bible relate to people of today just as much as they did to the people throughout the ages. We cannot and must not change the laws of God. That is why the test is faithfulness to the Word. Deviation from God's Word results in false teaching, apostasy, and backsliding.

Jesus then said, *"You have kept my word and have not denied my name,"* neither by your words or by your actions. You did not deny me even when you were ridiculed or insulted. Jesus told this church something interesting: their enemies would one day realize and admit that the church had been right.

At that time, Jesus protected the church of Philadelphia from a disaster, but He also spoke about the time of the great Tribulation, which He had mentioned in Matthew 24:21–24. It will come over the whole earth. He said that the church, which will have the nature of the church in Philadelphia, will be protected from this horrible time of Tribulation. He also said, *"I am coming soon!"* The church should be aware that Jesus will return soon.

NEITHER HOT
NOR COLD

REVELATION 3:14–22

"To the angel of the church in Laodicea write: These are the words of the Amen, the faithful and true witness, the ruler of God's creation. I know your deeds, that you are neither cold nor hot. I wish you were either one or the other! So, because you are lukewarm—neither hot nor cold—I am about to spit you out of my mouth. You say, 'I am rich; I have acquired wealth and do not need a thing.' But you do not realize that you are wretched, pitiful, poor, blind and naked. I counsel you to buy from me gold refined in the fire, so that you can become rich; and white clothes to wear, so that you can cover your shameful nakedness; and salve to put on your eyes, so that you can see. Those whom I love I rebuke and discipline. So be earnest, and repent. Here I am! I stand at the door and knock. If anyone hears my voice and opens the door, I will come in and eat with him, and he with me. To him who overcomes, I will give the right to sit with me on my throne, just as I overcame and sat down with my Father on his throne. He who has an ear, let him hear what the Spirit says to the churches."

The seven churches mentioned in the first three chapters of Revelation all had a similar beginning. Early in their development they received a scroll with implicit, God-inspired messages. In addition to this, they were taught verbally. Around the years 58–60 A.D., Paul sent letters to the churches in Colosse and Laodicea. The Bible tells us that he was very concerned about these churches. The letter to the Colossians was also to be read in Laodicea. We can read in Colossians 2:1, and then again in Colossians 4:13 and 16, that in his letter to the Colossians, Paul sends greetings to Laodicea. He mentions Epaphras who worked hard for the Laodiceans and who had a great inner burden for them.

All of these churches had a good beginning, yet barely thirty-five years after Paul had written these letters we can see vast differences in each of their developments. Of all the letters, this one to the church to Laodicea should interest us the most. Why? This is the letter which most closely resembles the church of the end time, and we are now living in the end time.

Laodicea was probably the most prosperous city at that time. We can see proof of this when the city, which was also destroyed by the earthquake around 60 B.C., refused all help from Rome for the rebuilding. They had sufficient financial means to rebuild on their own. On the hills surrounding Laodicea were springs of healing waters. People came from near and far to drink the hot water from these springs. The priests sold this water, which turned into a very profitable business. They mixed this water with healing herbs to produce an eye ointment, for which Laodicea was well known. The city was also very famous for the production of the latest fashion of clothing, especially those made from wool. The production of gold was also a lucrative business. Laodicea could be compared to modern-day London or Zurich. It also had a theatre which was larger than any temple, and even bigger than the arenas which were built during that time. Laodicea stood for, "justice by the people," "democracy," or "decisions made by the people." It appears that these ideas also crept into the church, not only into its leadership, but also into its spiritual attitude. To do just what the people wanted. The preaching was done to please.

Jesus introduced Himself as *"the Amen"* to this church, which had a good beginning and had the writings of Paul. Nowhere else in the Bible do we find that Jesus calls Himself *"the Amen."* Amen means, so be it. Paul wrote to the Corinthians that He is the Alpha and the Omega. In other words, Jesus said that whatever He says is true.

After He introduced Himself to the church in this manner, He rebuked them and told them, *"I know your deeds, that you are neither cold nor hot. I wish you were either one or the other! So, because you are lukewarm—neither hot nor cold, I am about to spit you out of my mouth."* This church had not always been like this. It had been different once! We know that such a decline does not happen overnight. As long as we adhere to God's Word, the devil does not come to us and tell us that creation is a lie, or that the Bible is not the Word of God. This happens over time. It begins with us wanting to understand, to reason, and to explain everything. However, the more that a person deviates from the Word and ways of God and relies on his own understanding to guide him, the result will be spiritual blindness and numbness.

Jesus refers to three spiritual levels. He speaks of people who are cold, hot or lukewarm. Someone cold is not in the Kingdom of God. Hot is someone who has repented, has accepted Jesus, and has been born again; he is convinced about God, about Jesus and about salvation. He knows that he is a child of God! He is united with Jesus and has an intimate relationship with God, the Father.

But Jesus tells them that this is not the case with this church. They are not "hot", nor are they people who do not know God. They are lukewarm. Jesus was referring to a situation that was well-known to the Laodiceans. Tacitus spoke of the springs of healing waters, whose springs had hot mineral water, which was drunk as medicine. It had a pleasant taste and many testified that they were healed by drinking it. Jesus said, "You are not hot." He was referring to the healing waters which flowed down the mountain. After flowing on a downward slope of approximately 150 meters, the water had become lukewarm. People who did not want to climb the mountain, and drank the lukewarm water, discovered that it had a horrible taste. They could not drink it and had to spit it out. It appeared that as the water cooled some kind of chemical process caused such a phenomenon. The amazing fact, as Tacitus reported, was that as the water continued to flow down and reached the bottom it became cold and was drinkable again. The Laodiceans knew what Jesus meant!

Jesus told the Laodiceans, and many since, that they resembled these healing waters which were not just undrinkable, but had to be spat out. It is true there is nothing more tragic than a lukewarm Christian! A Christian who is on fire for the Lord can be misunderstood, but he or she will be known as a follower of Jesus. The Lord points out, however, that many people living in the end time will be in this "lukewarm" situation, and will still think they are perfectly alright.

Their false self-evaluation leads them astray: *"I am rich; I have acquired wealth and do not need a thing."* Jesus told this church, and it counts for the people in our time, *"I counsel you to buy from me gold refined in the fire."* Gold that looked as if it were real was often sold, but it was not pure—it contained a mixture. When this was melted, many impurities which had been added to increase its mass appeared.

All of us will have to go through a refining process, like the gold—a trial by fire. The fire will reveal whether our Christianity was real, or whether it was mixed with worldliness. Only if our Christianity is genuine will we be able to meet God. Jesus said, *"Buy from me gold refined in the fire."* What is this gold? It is that which the Word of God and the Holy Spirit have achieved in our lives.

Jesus continued to say, *"Buy white clothes to wear, so you can cover your shameful nakedness."* You are standing before me and you look completely different to me. *"Buy salve to put on your eyes, so you can see."* Jesus was telling them to buy salve from Him so that their spiritual eyes would be opened. Whoever accepts Jesus by faith begins to have spiritual eyesight.

These people lived in apparent holiness without having any spiritual characteristics or spiritual life. Jesus pointed out the reason for this. They had left Him out of their lives and out of their church. He was not their Lord, nor did they have an intimate relationship with Him, which is absolutely essential. *"Here I am! I stand at the door and knock!"*

In his second letter to Timothy, Paul wrote that in the last days there will be people who will have love for themselves, for pleasure, and for money. They will be *"having a form of godliness but denying its power"* (2 Timothy 3:5). This also refers to the church in Laodicea. They gave the appearance of being Christians, but God's power and godly living was missing. Jesus stood knocking outside the door. They did not accept Him as their Lord. The intimate relationship was missing. They were able to give lectures about the Bible and about Jesus. They were knowledgeable about social events, human nature and humanism, and encouraged these things, but communion with Jesus was missing, and He was not their Lord. They were lukewarm, and Jesus said to them, *"I am about to spit you out of my mouth."* He said, *"Here I am! I stand at the door and knock."* He wants to get into your life and into your heart so that He can have fellowship with you and you with Him.

THE RAPTURE

Jesus told John that He would show him *"what is now and what will take place later."* In Revelation 2 and 3, John saw the condition of the churches at his time and in the future. After John saw all of this, he tells us in Revelation 4:1, *"There before me was a door standing open in heaven."* He was then told, *"come up here and I will show you what must take place after this."* He was then shown what would happen on earth after the end of the Dispensation of the Church. John testifies that his spirit was in Heaven.

According to the New Testament, which event will cause the end of the Dispensation of the Church? It is the Rapture!

The Bible speaks about this in 1 Thessalonians 4:16–17:

> *"For the Lord himself will come down from heaven, with a loud command, with the voice of the archangel and with the trumpet call of God, and the dead in Christ will rise first. After that, we who are still alive and are left will be caught up together with them in the clouds to meet the Lord in the air. And so we will be with the Lord forever."*

Also, in 1 Corinthians 15:51–53:

> *"Listen, I tell you a mystery: We will not all sleep, but we will all be changed—in a flash, in the twinkling of an eye, at the last trumpet. For the trumpet will sound the dead will be raised imperishable, and we will be changed. For the perishable must clothe itself with the imperishable and the mortal with immortality."*

Long before this was revealed to John, God told the church—and the disciples were told by Jesus—that they should watch and pray in order to be a part of that great event, the Rapture.

In Luke 21:36, Jesus admonishes the disciples with these words: *"Be always on the watch, and pray that you may be able to escape all that is about to happen, and that you may be able to stand before the Son of Man."* In Matthew 25:13, there is a similar reminder from Jesus. After He told the parable of the five foolish and the five wise virgins, He said, *"Therefore keep watch, because you do not know the day or hour."* Paul wrote to the Thessalonians and urged them in 1 Thessalonians 1:10 *"to wait for his Son from heaven."* The event which ends the Dispensation of the Church will be the Rapture. We must always be aware that the Bible does not give us a definite time when the Rapture will occur.

What is the Rapture?

The Rapture is the event when Jesus will come and this Dispensation will end. Not everyone will die; those who are still alive and believe that Jesus died and rose again will be changed in the twinkling of an eye, and the dead in Christ will be raised, and together they shall be taken up to be with Christ.

Our physical body cannot get to heaven and enter the Kingdom of God. Jesus said that this body has to be transfigured. We shall have a body like Jesus had after the Resurrection, a body which does not adhere to physical attributes. We read about this change of our bodies and the Rapture in 1 Thessalonians 4:15–17 and in 1 Corinthians 15:51–52.

At What Point in History Will the Rapture Take Place?

The more I study the Scriptures, the more I am convinced that there will not be just one Rapture. It seems to me that the Bible speaks of at least three groups who will be Raptured at different times.

One of these groups—those who overcome, as Jesus calls them in Revelation 2 and 3—will be taken away before the Tribulation. We read about another group which will be Raptured during the Tribulation.

And finally, we read about a group of one hundred and forty-four thousand who will be Raptured later.

It is clear that Jesus in His teachings, the Apostles in their letters, and then Jesus again in the letters to the churches, want to impress upon us that we should belong to the group of those who overcome. That is the group about which He says, *"To him who overcomes, I will give the right to sit with me on my throne, just as I overcame and sat down with my Father on His throne"* (Revelation 3:21).

Why am I of the opinion that the Rapture of those who overcome has already taken place in Revelation 4? Besides other facts, it is because we read about what John saw:

"Surrounding the throne were twenty-four other thrones, and seated on them were twenty-four elders. They were dressed in white and had crowns of gold on their heads. From the throne came flashes of lightning, rumblings and peals of thunder. Before the throne, seven lamps were blazing. These are the seven spirits of God. Also before the throne there was what looked like a sea of glass, clear as crystal" (Revelation 4:4–6a).

John saw God on the throne, and yet he did not see Him as He really was. He describes Him by comparing Him to glittering jewels. On one side was the Seat of Judgment—flashes of lightning, rumblings and peals of thunder are evidence of that. The other side was the Seat of Mercy, which the rainbow symbolizes. John saw something else. There were twenty-four thrones surrounding the throne, and seated on them were twenty-four elders with crowns of gold.

Daniel saw something similar to this in Daniel 7:9:

"As I looked, "thrones were set in place, and the Ancient of Days took his seat. His clothing was as white as snow; the hair of his head was white like wool. His throne was flaming with fire, and its wheels were all ablaze. A river of fire was flowing, coming out from before him. Thousands upon thousands attended him; ten thousand times ten thousand stood before him. The court was seated, and the books were opened."

Ezekiel also had an almost identical vision of the Throne of God. We read about this in Ezekiel 1 and 11. Both Daniel and Ezekiel saw the throne, the heavenly beings and the splendor around the throne. The throne Isaiah saw in Isaiah 6 was described in a similar way, but only John saw the elders. Why? Because the elders were not there in the previous times.

In the Bible, elders are leaders, people with responsibility to which God gave authority. John recognized that God had bestowed authority and responsibility upon those who sat on the thrones. He could find no other word to describe them except elders.

Who are these elders? I believe that the number twenty-four is just symbolic, that this is a specific group. We read about them in Revelation 5:9 and 10:

> "And they sang a new song, saying: "You are worthy to take the scroll, And to open its seals; For You were slain, And have redeemed us to God by Your blood Out of every tribe and tongue and people and nation, And have made us kings and priests to our God; And we shall reign on the earth" (NKJV).

If they come from every tribe, language, people and nation, they must be a very large group, not just twenty-four. There is some disagreement if the translation in chapter 5:10 should say "us" or "they." The Codex Siniaticus, the Coptic, Armenian, and Latin manuscripts all use "we" as well as the Codex Basilianus. The exception is the Codex Alexandrinus. It seems to me that the twenty-four elders represent the group of people of which Jesus said, "To him who overcomes, I will give the right to sit with me on my throne, just as I overcame and sat down with my Father on His throne" (Revelation 3:21). They have been Raptured before the great Tribulation.

Another reason why I believe the elders are the redeemed people who have been Raptured is that the Bible says they have crowns on their heads and are clothed in white gowns. Only people who are redeemed and have been validated by the Lord receive crowns, and only those who have been washed in the blood of Jesus have white gowns. Angels are holy beings, but they receive neither crowns from God nor the white robes of the redeemed.

John was shown something neither Ezekiel, Daniel, nor Isaiah saw or were not able to see. They saw the throne of God and the living beings as they honored and worshiped God. John was now shown that a group of elders was there. These were not there previously because the Overcomers, the bride of Jesus, were not yet there.

The heavenly beings continue to perform their duties, but while they are saying, "Holy, holy, holy," the group of Overcomers stand and lay their crowns before Him who sits on the throne. Then they stand, fall down before Him and worship Him, "You are worthy to receive glory and honor and power." They place their crowns down, knowing that they do not deserve them, but that they actually belong to Him because He was slain, and with His blood He purchased them for God. Even so, He gave them the crowns and elevated them by placing them on thrones! Jesus has chosen all of us for such a destiny.

A WOMAN CLOTHED WITH THE SUN, THE CHILD AND THE DRAGON

REVELATION 12:1—17

U p to chapter 11, Revelation gives us a description of things that will happen up to the fulfillment of the secrets of God. Verse 15 says, *"The kingdom of the world has become the kingdom of our Lord and of his Christ, and he will reign forever and ever."*

I have already mentioned that I think John received two visions of the events that will happen. If chapter 11 concludes the chronological order of John's first vision, where does chapter 12 begin?

My understanding is that, chronologically, Revelation 12 can be placed just before the end of the Dispensation of the Church, and just before the appearance of the antichrist.

The question that concerns us is who is this woman? Some explain her to be Israel, the church, or the city of Jerusalem. Others perceive her as Mary. It is important to remember Jesus told John that what he sees concerns future events.

There are certain references in the Bible which seem to indicate that this woman refers to Israel, and that the child who is mentioned here is Jesus. The nation of Israel is often referred to as a woman. After Jesus' birth, He lived on earth, died, was resurrected and Raptured into heaven. In John 12:31, we read that when Jesus comes, the prince of this world will be driven out. This we also find in Revelation. In Psalms 2, 8 and 9, the Bible tells us that Jesus will come and will rule with an iron scepter. That is why some are convinced that this woman is Israel and the baby is Jesus. However, John is speaking about things that will happen in the future. When he had this vision, Jesus had already been born and was already up in heaven with His father.

Notice that verses 7–12 say that a battle with the dragon, the devil, will occur, and that he will be hurled from heaven unto earth. In Ephesians 6:12 we read, *"Our struggle is not against flesh and blood, but against the rulers, against the authorities, against the powers of this dark world and against the spiritual forces of evil in the heavenly realms."* Do you notice something here? When Satan, in conjunction with this woman and her child, will be hurled to earth, it will be in the future. At present, he is residing in heavenly regions. He exercises his power upon earth, but for now he still has access to God as an accuser of the believers. He will only be forced from the heavenly regions at the end of the aforementioned battle. At that time, he will lose his position as accuser. It is also mentioned in this text that the dragon knows that once he has been hurled to the earth, he has very little time available. He will wage war against other offspring of the woman.

Who is this woman? This woman has her beginnings in the prophecy found in Genesis 3:15, where God says, *"And I will put enmity between you and the woman, and between your offspring and hers."* I see her to be Christianity.

Who is this child and when will this child be born? In Revelation 12:3, we read about the *"other"* sign. One sign was the woman, the other was the dragon. This was an enormous red dragon with seven heads and ten horns and seven crowns on his heads. These horns did not have crowns, at least not in this chapter; however, in chapter 13, we read then that the horns have crowns.

Almost all Biblical scholars agree about the following. The seven heads are the seven world empires, beginning with the Egyptian, Assyrian, Babylonian, Persian, Greek, Roman, and the reign of the antichrist. The Bible states that these seven heads, or these seven empires, are crowned, or have already come to power. The union of ten nations, which is supposed to appear, is at this time not yet crowned. Later, in chapter 13, when the antichrist appears and comes to power, it will be crowned. From this, I conclude that the moment when this occurs will be at the end of the Dispensation of the church, before the Tribulation.

But who is this child? The Bible says that he will rule the heathen nations with an iron rod, and he will be Raptured to God, and to His throne. We read in Revelation 2:26–27:

"To him who overcomes and does my will to the end, I will give authority over the nations—'He will rule them with an iron scepter; he will dash them to pieces like pottery'—just as I have received authority from my Father."

In the same chapter, the church in Thyatira is warned that those who do not overcome will suffer and will be paid according to their deeds. Therefore, it must refer to the group of Overcomers, those who will be Raptured, those who will be sitting with Jesus on His throne, and those who have received crowns and who will be reigning with Him. We also see them in another Biblical picture. It will be those who belong to the group of the wise virgins, the children of God who await the coming of Jesus, who love the coming of Jesus, and who are Overcomers.

I think Paul shared this opinion. In Philippians 3, he leads one to think he had become uncertain about his spiritual position. He says that he has not achieved something. He says that he wants to be a part of the resurrection of the dead, giving the impression that he is unsure whether he will be part of it. Did Paul suddenly doubt his salvation and whether he would rise from the dead? Is Paul even discussing salvation here? I believe not!

Paul was the one who taught the churches about the plan of salvation. He is the one who wrote, *"I know in whom I believe!"* He was so convincing when he wrote to the Corinthians about the resurrection of the dead. We can deduce that Paul was certain of his salvation and of being a Christian. He said, *"I have fought a good fight; I know where I am going."* He had a definite knowledge about being a child of God and he preached clearly that everyone who belongs to Jesus is a child of God. Was he suddenly uncertain of this? Absolutely not!

Paul knew he was a child of God; he knew he would someday be with Jesus, but he was not certain whether he would be among the group of Overcomers. He said that he is striving toward this, and is doing everything possible to be counted among them. He also knew that he would rise from the dead. Yet in Philippians 3:11, it seems he is in doubt. What does he speak about in this verse? Not the resurrection of believers in general. The Greek word for resurrection in verse 11 gives the meaning of a resurrection that comes out of, or before, this general resurrection of all believers.

Does this mean not every believer will be Raptured before the Tribulation? I believe so. There is so much which indicates that not all believers will be present at the Rapture before the Tribulation. That is why we always find these words of our Lord in the seven letters to the churches, *"...to him who overcomes."* That is why Jesus urges in Luke 21:36, *"Be always on the watch, and pray that you may be able to escape all that is about to happen."*

This twelfth chapter also discusses the dragon, which we know to be the devil. Since his rebellion against God, he has been God's enemy. He will try his utmost to prevent this child, the group of Overcomers, being Raptured to God. There will be a turbulent battle, and God will have to send in Michael the Archangel. The devil will be there with all of his angels. Just imagine this scene. The entire army of hell will be summoned to go against the people of God, those who surrendered their lives to Him. The Bible says that Michael will fight on behalf God's people, but that the Overcomers will also have a part in the victory. They will defeat the devil through the blood of the Lamb, by the words of their testimonies, and by the complete submission of their lives to God. Oh, for the power of the blood and the power of the Word and its testimony!

As a result of this Rapture, the devil and all his angels will be hurled to the earth. I believe that this will be the beginning of the

Tribulation here on earth. The devil knows that there is only a short period of time allowed to him. What will he do? His battle will be directed toward the remaining offspring of this woman, the remaining believers. When the Tribulation begins, a part of the church of Jesus, a part of God's children, will have suddenly vanished. The Bible says that the remaining believers, those who were left behind, will begin to flee to places where they hope to be safe from the enemy. That will cause quite an exodus from certain countries. They will try to escape, and the dragon will fight against the children of God who have remained on earth. The Bible says that many of these will die a martyr's death. The devil will use his entire power to eradicate the believers on earth. Even if he succeeds in killing many of the believers, he will not be able to achieve his ultimate goal to become supreme ruler of this earth. The Bible says he is defeated! Joyful tidings will be shouted in heaven: *"The kingdom of the world has become the kingdom of our Lord and of his Christ, and he will reign forever and ever."*

THE SEALED SCROLL

John was still standing before the throne he had described in chapter 4. As he was observing it, he noticed a scroll that was held in the hand of the One who sat on the throne. John knew immediately that there was something extraordinary about this scroll. He looked at it more intensely and noticed that it was sealed with seven seals.

The custom of sealing, which was prevalent in the Old Testament, is hardly known today. Important documents and special property mortgages used to be sealed with seals. The writer wrote on a parchment scroll or a roll of papyrus. After he wrote a portion of the document, it would be rolled up and sealed with the first seal. He would continue writing until the second seal was used, and would continue to do so until the whole document had been sealed.

When the nation of Israel entered the Promised Land, it was told to pay attention to how the land was to be divided. Each family received a portion. It was God's intent that this land should always remain with the family who received it and should never be taken away from them. However, it happened that some, due to debts, had to mortgage or even sell their land. God did not want the land to remain in foreign hands, and thus he gave them a wonderful and interesting law. If a property had to be mortgaged or sold, it had to written up on a scroll and sealed. At the same time, an unsealed letter of purchase was also written up. As soon as the said party was able to re-purchase his deeded land, the sealed copy was opened. Inside were written the conditions required to buy back the property and have it returned to the family to whom it was originally given. In Bible times, this property was said to be redeemed, which leads to the expression *the redeemer*. Only a member of the original family to whom God had designated the land was able to redeem it back from someone who had legally attained the land.

We can see here an interesting occurrence. At a specific time, Jeremiah knew that the land would be conquered, and that captivity would last another seventy years. A property had been given to his family, and was supposed to remain in the family. In Jeremiah 32, we read that he redeemed this land even though he was not yet able to take ownership. A sale document was signed and the scroll was sealed. Jeremiah put the sealed scroll into a clay pot in order to keep it safe. After the time of captivity, when the people went back to their own land, his descendants would have the rightful ownership of this land, the land for which he had already paid the required price.

The scroll with the seven seals must have had a tremendous significance; otherwise John would not have cried so bitterly. It relates to the guilt of the people when they separated and removed themselves from God. When God made man, He made him wonderfully. The Bible says that all God made was good. He made man and set him on earth. He wanted man to be ruler over the earth and everything in it. At that time, man lived in an untroubled relationship with God.

But man rebelled against God. He did not want to have someone ruling over him. The snake, the devil, told man, *"For God knows that when you eat of [the tree of knowledge of good and evil] your eyes will be opened, and you will be like God, knowing good and evil"* (Genesis 3:5). Man did not want to be subjected to someone ruling over him. At that moment, man lost the Glory that God had given him. As a result, sin came into his life, followed by sickness and another consequence, which is still very evident today, death. All trouble, sorrow and much more than I could name became a part of this.

That was not all. Because man disobeyed God, he not only revoked God's sovereignty over himself, but delivered the whole earth to the devil. Many people ask, "Why is there so much tragedy in this world?" We know why, because now the devil is the ruler of the earth. In Luke 4:6–7, when Satan showed Jesus all of the kingdoms of the world, he said to Jesus, *"I will give you all their authority and splendor, for it has been given to me, and I can give it to anyone I want to. So if you worship me, it will all be yours."* This would not have been a temptation for Jesus if this had not been true.

That is the reason for so many evil things happening on earth up to this day. Many people blame God. Man lost so much; through his own fault he mortgaged himself and all the earth. This scroll was about this, and everything was carefully documented in it.

The redemption Jesus fulfilled had to include everything man lost, as well as the return to the Glory he had with God, and the restoration of authority over the earth. Who can save man from this debt of his own causing? It has to be someone without any debt, someone who can pay the price, someone from the family, and it has to be a person.

Now we can understand John's reaction as he turned around and found no one worthy to open the scroll. No one, no person, no angel, no one! It was no wonder John cried. He knew if this scroll could not be opened and the seals not broken, the earth would remain under the rule of Satan forever.

Then he heard the most wonderful words: *"Do not weep! See, the Lion of the tribe of Judah, the Root of David, has triumphed. He is able to open the scroll and the seven seals"* (Revelation 5:5b–6). John saw Him, the Lion, as the Lamb! He was the man without fault and without debt. He put aside His divinity. He did not insist on keeping His godliness, as we would if we won something so extravagant. He had every right to do so, but instead He gave up His godliness and became man. He identified Himself with us in order to be counted as one of our family, and He paid the full price of redemption with His own blood, in order to redeem us.

The moment had arrived when the scroll would be opened. The complete debt, brought about by the sinning of man, has been repaid by Jesus. Just as Jeremiah had paid the price, even though the owners did not yet take ownership of the property, Jesus paid the price on Golgotha, even though the opening of the scroll would take place many years later. The price has been paid!

When will this take place? It will be after the Dispensation of the Church has ended. Have you ever asked yourself what is so important about the church? It is in the church where we are to practice living in the same manner as God had expected Adam and Eve to do before they sinned. We are to voluntarily submit ourselves to our Father, to follow Him, to acknowledge His Lordship over us and to live accordingly.

The Bible also refers to Christians as children of the Kingdom of God. They are the ones who have voluntarily accepted the sovereign authority of Jesus Christ, and do not declare, "I live my own life, no one can tell me what to do; I'll do it my way!" They are the ones who have submitted to Jesus and His godly thoughts, and who are now in the church in order to become better acquainted with God, to serve Him and to follow Him.

The world has always done as it wants. It says, "No one will control me!" People who belong to the church must and should acknowledge the supremacy of God. Those who do so will belong to the Overcomers and will be taken from this world up to the throne of God, after the Dispensation of the Church. The moment will arrive when everything man lost through the fall will be restored, and it will be the beginning of a tremendous, dramatic pageant.

As John was viewing this, he noticed that the elders were holding golden bowls full of incense; these are the prayers of the saints. This is verification of how important our prayers are. Have we not often thought our prayers were in vain? How did Jesus teach us to pray? *"Our Father in heaven, hallowed be your name, your kingdom come…"* (Matthew 6:9–10) It will come, and soon. How often have we prayed, "Let your kingdom come?" These prayers are not lost.

During this vision, John experienced a worship service before God's throne. The four living creatures and the elders worshipped and praised God and the Lamb, and with them thousands upon thousands and ten thousand times ten thousand angels. We cannot comprehend how many that would be. These are millions of angels. Notice they are not standing where the redeemed, the Overcomers, are. The angels join them in their song, but they themselves have never experienced redemption.

The angels had experienced what it meant to the Father when man rebelled against Him and brought about this debt. They had also experienced how much it cost the Son to give up His majesty. They experienced how the Father turned His face away from Jesus as Jesus took all the sins of mankind upon Himself. Now they could personally witness how all of this had been worthwhile, and they joined in the worship and praise. For whom is this? The person who is receiving this adoration is Jesus, the Lamb. He is the one about whom is said,

"Worthy is the Lamb, who was slain, to receive power and wealth and wisdom and strength and honor and glory and praise" (Revelation 5:12). There, before the throne of God, we shall not be able to do anything else except raise our hands and voices to worship and praise. Some people have difficulty doing this now. The more we acknowledge what He has done, the more we realize that: He is worthy! Honor, glory, worship and praise will reverberate throughout heaven. Are we already able to worship and praise him?

There will be people who attended church, who knew everything, and yet will not be among the Rapture. There will be people who were raised as Christians, who at one time had given their lives to God, who had started to live for God, but will belong to the five foolish virgins, and will not take part in this worship service in front of God's throne when the Lamb will take the scroll and open it. They did not submit to Jesus' lordship. They are not Overcomers! They had taken charge of their own lives.

THE OPENING
OF THE SEALS

I n Revelation 5, we get the impression that it was not possible to open the scroll with the seven seals until the group the Bible calls the elders has been removed from earth. We find this group in front of God's throne, and in chapter 6, we find that Jesus, the Lamb, is beginning to open the seals.

We read that one of the four living creatures said, *"Come."* John saw a white horse whose rider held a bow, was given a crown and rode out as a conqueror, bent on conquest. Who is this man on the white horse?

Some believe it is Jesus, because in Revelation 19 it also speaks of a white horse, and the one sitting on it is, without doubt, Jesus. And yes, it is at this time that Jesus will begin His triumphant possession of the earth. However, the white horse in chapter 6 and the rider on it, as far as I understand it, is very closely connected to the other horses and riders described further on. I also think that Jesus Himself refers to these four riders in Mathew 24:4-7. From this, we can better understand the interpretation. Let us pay close attention to what the verses say when He was asked the question, when would this happen and what would be the signs of His return?

"Watch out that no one deceives you. For many will come in my name, claiming, 'I am the Christ,' and will deceive many. You will hear of wars and rumors of wars, but see to it that you are not alarmed. Such things must happen, but the end is still to come. Nation will rise against nation, and kingdom against kingdom. There will be famines and earthquakes in various places."

Jesus mentions four things here: deception through false Messiahs, wars and rumors of wars, famines, and death due to pestilence and earthquakes. Let us look then at the four riders. They depict exactly what Jesus was describing here. The rider on the white horse is clearly the antichrist going out to deceive. Daniel spoke about the antichrist in Daniel 9; he said that he would come in peace. This is depicted by the white horse. He will appear on the world stage as a man of peace. He will make a treaty with Israel. He will have the support of the world church, and it will be said that here is the man who will bring peace to the earth, and who is able to solve earth's problems. It will not take long before he reveals his true identity. He will break the treaty with Israel, and later he will destroy the world church. Revelation 17 speaks of all of this.

When the antichrist has assumed power, the events mentioned as the second seal is opened will take place. The Bible says that there was another horse, a fiery red one, and its rider was given power to take peace from the earth and to cause men to slay each other. To him was given a large sword. His appearance will cause a great celebration, and soon afterward he will attack those who do not accept his power.

The Bible shows that the third rider will appear on a black horse and he will hold a pair of scales in his hand to weigh food. War will cause a great economic crisis. There will be a shortage of food, especially the most essential items. There will be a huge rise in the cost of living, and it will be necessary to work one whole day in order to buy bread. Just imagine what this means! The black market will bloom, and there will be hunger and want. This is already evident in many countries today. The Bible does show us that there will be some who will still have more than enough. There will be some who still have ample oil and wine, depicting a picture of surplus. The Word of God tells us that the economic crisis will be so terrible that a system of rationing will have to be set in place. The horrible part of this will be that only those who have accepted the antichrist will be permitted to buy and sell.

Why does the antichrist connect buying and selling with the acceptance or refusal of himself and of his position? He will find opposition here on earth. Some will stand and give warning about this man. There will be those who will preach against him and will claim that he is the false Christ. He will try to destroy them by combining the conditions of buying and selling with the acceptance of him and of his power. Those who do not comply will be put to death.

The Bible shows us what will happen after this. When the fourth seal was opened, a pale horse appeared. Its rider was Death. The Bible tells us there will be a time of many deaths on this earth. At the time of the opening of the fourth seal, a fourth of the earth's population will die. When the Bible talks about the time of the opening of the seals, it is speaking of the great Tribulation, a time such as the earth has never seen.

Let us look at the fifth seal. The Bible tells us that when the Lamb opened the fifth seal, John saw the souls of those who had been slain because of the Word of God and the testimony they had maintained, under the altar:

> *"They called out in a loud voice, 'How long, Sovereign Lord, holy and true, until you judge the inhabitants of the earth and avenge our blood?' Then each of them was given a white robe, and they were told to wait a little longer, until the number of their fellow servants and brothers who were to be killed as they had been was completed"* (Revelation 6:10–11).

John saw a multitude, not around the throne, but under it.

We know of the parable of the ten virgins in Matthew 25. What is written there? When the call came that the bridegroom had arrived, five were ready, but five had to go out to buy oil. The five who were ready went to the wedding feast with the bridegroom. When the five foolish virgins returned, they too wanted to enter the wedding feast, but the bridegroom replied, *"I tell you the truth, I don't know you"*

(Matthew 25:12). From this, we can see that all ten went out together. All ten had at one time experienced salvation and all ten at one time had some oil. At the time when the bridegroom arrived, the foolish did not have enough oil, and only five went along as the bride. This bride is the wise virgins, the ones in front of the throne. They experience the opening of the seals by the Lamb. The five foolish virgins remain behind on earth when the bridegroom arrives.

My dear readers, do you understand what the Bible is saying? Are the ones who are left behind now lost? They do not have to be lost, but they will never belong to the bride. The bride of Jesus is Raptured, and those who belong to the foolish virgins are left behind when the antichrist begins his reign on earth. Then many of them will recognize the truth of God's Word, and they will know what has happened. They will recognize the one who appears as the man of peace, and will say, "This is no peacemaker, this is the antichrist," and then they will—thank God—look to the Word of God. However, many of them will be persecuted and tortured, and many will be put to death.

These are the people John saw under the altar, and about whom Jesus said there were still many on the earth, and they would be executed because of the Word of God. The Word of God will still be preached, even at the beginning of the antichrist's reign. There will be those who did not take God's Word seriously, did not obey Jesus and the Word of God, and thought that, as Christians, they could live as they pleased. They will suddenly wake up and realize the truth. However, they will not be a part of the bride.

How many people are at this moment playing with their salvation? They have often heard the voice of God and have experienced the call of God through the scriptures, but have no inner fire burning for Jesus. They love the things of the world much more than they love Jesus. Their desires and pleasures are much more important than being obedient to Jesus. Recognition by people is much more important to them than recognition by God. Jesus calls them, He asks them, to reach out to Him and to obey His Word, but they do not take this seriously. He asks them to live holy lives, but they do not respond, and they fool around with their spirituality. They put off for tomorrow the things that they should do today. They always want to serve God later, to take things more seriously later, to break off from sin another day, to stop bad habits in the future, and they will not do it today. When Jesus arrives and the call goes out, "The bridegroom is coming!" it will be too late.

I fear that even during this time many will not be able to withstand the great pressure that the children of God will experience during the time of Tribulation. However, many people will realize what they had neglected, and they will search for God. They will be saved, but the Bible says it will be like going through fire. They will not belong to the bride, and they will not receive a crown. Jesus is now giving us such a wonderful opportunity to completely commit our lives to Him.

Dear friends, understanding the seals being able to interpret all of the mysteries in Revelation is not important as an end in itself, but only as a means of understanding what is of utmost importance—that we maintain our personal relationship with Jesus, and obey the Lamb of God. This is what counts. Some people always want to study. They spend time with pictures and models and they go to great efforts to discover minute details. This is not important, *unless* it is used to help in our relationship with the Lamb, with Jesus.

We must never preach that once you are saved and born again everything will be fine, just as we cannot say that when a child is born this is all there is to a life. It is just the beginning, an important beginning, a definite beginning. The Bible does not say that the beginning will be crowned. It says that he who overcomes until the end will be crowned. Do you understand this?

Do we ask ourselves, "Will this happen soon?" The Bible tells us that no one knows the time or the hour. God's Word indicates that the children of God, who belong to the bride, will not be surprised when Jesus comes (1 Thessalonians 5:4). Those who have no intimate relationship with Jesus, who are in darkness, will be surprised.

Will He come soon? Ask a true Christian. Let us look at the signs of the time. Ask any child of God, who has a close relationship with Jesus, and he will say that he senses by God's Spirit that Jesus will soon return. There are various signs depicting this. So much of what we see in today's political scene is a preparation for the moment when the antichrist will arrive.

The time span between the appearance of the antichrist and the moment when John saw the people under the altar will not even be a decade. It will happen very quickly. The Bible tells us a great multitude will be killed because of the Word of God. God gives us the opportunity to completely surrender our lives to Jesus *now*, to accept Him as our Lord and Savior and to live under His Lordship.

THE SIXTH SEAL

The Tribulation will be a hard time for the Christians who have remained on earth and for those who will turn to Christ only then. People who will be possessed by the devil will plague, persecute and torture the Christians, and yet there will still be opportunity to attain salvation. This will be very difficult, and many people will have to die the death of a martyr. This will be a time when the devil, with the help of people, will fight outright against God and anything that is godly on this earth. Revelation 13:1–18 give further insights about the antichrist.

Besides being a person, the antichrist is a system and an empire. Some find it very difficult to combine these three, and yet it must be done. The early Christians knew about the antichrist. This is not a doctrine which appeared later in the church. The first church was already taught about the antichrist, as John wrote in 1 John 2:18, "*...as you have heard that the antichrist is coming, even now many antichrists have come.*"

Are there many, or is there only one antichrist? In reality, there is only one, but there are many forerunners. There are many who have adopted his nature and to some extent impersonate him and display his character. Paul wrote in 2 Thessalonians 2:3–4:

> "*Don't let anyone deceive you in any way, for that day will not come until the rebellion occurs and the man of lawlessness is revealed, the man doomed to destruction. He will oppose and will exalt himself over everything that is called God or is*

worshiped, so that he sets himself up in God's temple, proclaiming himself to be God."

It is not difficult to comprehend that in order for the antichrist to be able to make his debut, there will have to be a definite time of preparation so that everything will be ready for him. This has always been the case with every event. The time had to be ripe, even for the coming of Jesus. Much of the happenings in the Old Testament can be seen as preparation for Jesus' arrival. In the Old Testament, we read about many men of God who make definite references to Jesus. The entire development of the Old Testament culminates with the fact that Jesus, the Messiah, will come. The Bible tells us, *"And when the time was fulfilled, God sent His Son"* (Galatians 4:4). After Jesus went back to his Father, there was an entirely different course of development. The earth had to be prepared so that the antichrist could arrive. On the other side, there is a much nicer development, and that is the preparation of the church of Jesus. However, in a world without God, the development continues and will culminate in the coming of the antichrist. That is why I call it a system.

Since Jesus' time on earth, there have been a number of people who were, and are, types, or forerunners, of the antichrist. The actual antichrist has not yet made his appearance, but he will come. He has had many forerunners in several systems, but we have always noted that from time to time God sent revivals of His power, glory, and victory through His church. God restrained the development of the antichrist's system. Why? It is because God is merciful, and in His loving kindness He wishes that everyone be saved.

In Revelation 13, we read about the beast coming out of the sea. The beast is the antichrist. Revelation 17 explains this very clearly. There we read that the antichrist comes from the multitudes, from the nations. He is a person, but his strength and power will come from the devil.

Six hundred years before John saw this vision on Patmos, Daniel received this revelation from God in Daniel 7:19–27:

"Then I wanted to know the true meaning of the fourth beast, the one so different from the others and so terrifying. It had

devoured and crushed its victims with iron teeth and bronze claws, trampling their remains beneath its feet. I also asked about the ten horns on the fourth beast's head and the little horn that came up afterward and destroyed three of the other horns. This horn had seemed greater than the others, and it had human eyes and a mouth that was boasting arrogantly. As I watched, this horn was waging war against God's holy people and was defeating them, until the Ancient One—the Most High—came and judged in favor of his holy people. Then the time arrived for the holy people to take over the kingdom. Then he said to me, 'This fourth beast is the fourth world power that will rule the earth. It will be different from all the others. It will devour the whole world, trampling and crushing everything in its path. Its ten horns are ten kings who will rule that empire. Then another king will arise, different from the other ten, who will subdue three of them. He will defy the Most High and oppress the holy people of the Most High. He will try to change their sacred festivals and laws, and they will be placed under his control for a time, times, and half a time. But then the court will pass judgment, and all his power will be taken away and completely destroyed. Then the sovereignty, power, and greatness of all the kingdoms under heaven will be given to the holy people of the Most High. His kingdom will last forever, and all rulers will serve and obey him.'"

Daniel had absolutely no conception of the church. How very courageous he was to write down these things, which he could not comprehend. John's courage is just as commendable! Both recognized from whom they received their messages.

We now live in a time when we can understand many of these things; firstly, because God's spirit reveals them, and secondly, because many of these things are happening in our time. The antichrist will come from the human race. He will be the head of the union of ten nations. The Bible indicates that at first three of these nations will oppose him and will not want him. Eventually, they will submit to him, accept him and acknowledge him as their leader. He will present solutions that promise many results. He will come and tell the people they need not violence, but peace, tranquility and order, and that they must have enough to eat. The Bible tells us that his power and wisdom come from the devil.

The Word of God mentions at the onset that when this man appears, he will suffer a wound—I do not speculate as to how—so terrible that the people will think he is dead. The Bible refers to it as a fatal wound. His recovery will be spectacular, completely confusing the people. He will probably claim that a higher power has sent him and has now helped him. The Bible tells us that people will worship this higher power, his god, the devil himself.

The Bible says in 2 Thessalonians 2:11-12, *"For this reason God sends them a powerful delusion so that they will believe the lie and so that all will be condemned who have not believed the truth but have delighted in wickedness."* Do you realize that these elements already exist in our society? I do not just mean the actual "churches" which admit to serving the devil, but I am thinking about the thousands of young people who, perhaps unknowingly, worship the devil through their music. Some bands have been said to have made pacts with the devil with apparently one goal in mind, to introduce devil worship. There are concerts where appeals are made to accept the devil. The greatest thing the devil longs for is worshippers. He tried it in the Garden of Eden, and then with Jesus when he told Him: *"All this I will give you, he said, if you will bow down and worship me."* Jesus refused! Now he tries to get people to worship him, the submission which belongs only to God our creator, and which only He should have. This is the devil's greatest priority.

Let us try to visualize how it will be on earth when the antichrist appears. The Rapture of the bride will have taken place. Many will discuss this event. The people who only believe what can actually be seen will try to deny the happening of the Rapture, but it will be a worldwide, undeniable and unambiguous event. Many people will have disappeared, especially those who had always talked about it. Jesus taught us to be prepared when he will come to take us to Himself. Due to the so-called miracle healing of the antichrist's wound, the sensation and discussion of the Rapture will become secondary. The antichrist will suddenly claim to be the "Savior" and will say, "Look, I have the power." This is the devil's ultimate aim. The Bible tells us that he will blaspheme against God, against those who live in heaven, and against those who were Raptured. He will ridicule them, and tell them that those things of which they spoke are not right, and that he has the power of God, which has been revealed through him. According to the Bible, he will become a powerful man on the earth, and the majority of people will accept him, trust him, and listen to him.

In Revelation 13, we read about a second beast coming out of the earth. The antichrist will require a religion, but not one just based on following rules. He will require a religion surrounded with miracles. The Bible tells us that another man will appear who will be his prophet. The devil wants to copy God in all matters. God sent His Son, who died and rose again. He became the Savior of all mankind, and when He ascended into heaven, He sent the Holy Spirit. The Holy Trinity is, up to this day, totally involved in the salvation and help of mankind. The dragon will send his antichrist, will let him go through an apparent death, will bring him back to life, and will give him a prophet as his mouthpiece to represent this diabolic trinity.

What kind of responsibilities will this prophet have? Just as it is the duty of the Holy Spirit to magnify Jesus, so it will be the duty of this prophet to honor the antichrist and to perform signs and miracles. Is the devil able to do this? The Bible even says that he will let fire fall from heaven. Just think of the time in the Old Testament when Moses received the commission to lead the Israelites out of Egypt. Remember the miracles and signs Egypt's magicians performed, which caused Pharaoh to harden his heart? There is good power and there is evil power. The antichrist's prophet will honor him and entice the people to serve the antichrist. He will erect a statue of the antichrist, which will have to be worshipped. He will demand total commitment to the antichrist. In order to monitor this, he will require each person to have a mark, either on the hands or on the forehead, to indicate dedication to the antichrist. Those who do not accept this mark will starve, and will not be able to buy or sell. If one should go to the supermarket or the bakery to buy bread, and not have this mark, he will not get any bread. If a child is sent to the store to buy milk, and does not have this mark, he or she will not get any milk.

Many people are worried about the number system, which we already have. When this mark is required, it will be connected to honoring and submitting to the antichrist. Today's developments in the number system, which are used for good and simplify our daily transactions, will be used by the antichrist for his evil purposes.

It will probably be an invisible number that can only be read by a scanner. It will not be evident just by sight. The prophet will try everything possible to induce people to completely submit to the antichrist. Those who do not will experience hard times. I am afraid that during those times there will be people who, having been influenced by the corruption of life in our time, will make compromises.

Another thing about those times is that not everything will run according to the antichrist's plan. Who will still be on the earth during this period? There will be many Christians who did not belong to the bride, those who did not have enough oil in their lamps. They will wake up and will want to make their stand for Jesus Christ. They will still be on earth. There will also be the one hundred and forty-four thousand sealed from the nation of Israel. They will be on earth. There will be two witnesses in Jerusalem, who will also be on earth. All of these will expose the antichrist, and will preach that he is a false Christ. They will be a thorn in his flesh, and there will be massive persecution. The Bible says that none of the believers would remain alive if God did not shorten this time. The antichrist will be furious that he will not succeed in bringing these people under his control, and will not be able to annihilate them completely.

The Rapture Out of the Tribulation—The Great Multitude in White Robes

In Revelation 7:9–16, we read that there will be a multitude of people who will be Raptured during the Tribulation. We notice that John was not able to identify these people. He could not place them. The only reason we know this today is because the Bible tells us. Verses 9–17 speak about a huge multitude that no one could count. When the fifth seal was opened, there was a great number of people under God's throne and they were calling out, *"How long, Sovereign Lord, holy and true, until you judge the inhabitants of the earth and avenge our blood"*

(Revelation 6:10)? They were from every nation, tribe, people and language. The Bible tells us that they came out of the great Tribulation.

We notice that there will be Christians in the Tribulation, and during the time of the Tribulation, salvation will still be possible. However, if there was ever a time when Christians had to endure persecution, it will be during the Tribulation.

I would like us to pay close attention to something. The people Raptured out of the Tribulation do not belong to the elite of the redeemed, the top of God's order. The Bible says that they will have palm branches and white robes. As far as the robe is concerned, one could interpret that they belong to the Overcomers; however, they do not have any crowns nor sit on thrones.. They follow the twenty-four elders who belong to a different order. The elders are royal priests who sit on thrones. The ones who come out of the Tribulation are servants before God's throne, and they will serve Him night and day.

I may be distorting the incorrect assumption of some Christians when I say that not every believer will be crowned ruler. We realize this from reading chapter 7. We cannot expect to live an indifferent Christian life and then, at the last minute, should we still be saved, have God put us in the same hierarchy as those who served Him with total submission. As far as I can see, John was of the opinion that everyone would be Raptured and would be with God before the Tribulation. He had no difficulty in identifying the elders, and understanding what else he saw. He seemingly had not known there would be Christians who would come out of the Tribulation. This was now revealed to him.

I am so thankful that this opportunity for salvation will still exist at that point. Jesus earnestly encourages us to endeavor to be part of the group who will be Raptured before Tribulation time. The biggest blessing a Christian can have is to belong to the group of conquerors, to the bride of Christ, to hear the call, to be ready, and not to be found asleep.

All of us should allow God's Word to shake us up, to help us realize the serious nature of our time, and to submit our lives totally to God. The Bible tells us to heed the message of the seven letters, and to become Overcomers. Only those who have overcome will be ready to heed the call of the bridegroom and go with Him to the wedding feast of the Lamb.

The Day of the Wrath of God

Besides the great Tribulation, the Bible also talks about the great day of the wrath of God. This is when the earth will receive judgments sent by God, aimed at the antichrist and an ungodly world. Don't ever believe that God cannot be angry! When the time of grace is completely over, God will send His wrath upon this earth.

According to my understanding, the day of the wrath of God is what has been mentioned in Zephaniah 1:14–18:

"The great day of the Lord is near—near and coming quickly. Listen! The cry on the day of the Lord will be bitter, the shouting of the warrior there. That day will be a day of wrath, a day of distress and anguish, a day of trouble and ruin, a day of darkness and gloom, a day of clouds and blackness, a day of trumpet and battle cry against the fortified cities and against the corner towers. I will bring distress on the people and they will walk like blind men, because they have sinned against the Lord. Their blood will be poured out like dust and their entrails like filth. Neither their silver nor their gold will be able to save them on the day of the Lord's wrath. In the fire of his jealousy the whole world will be consumed, for he will make a sudden end of all who live in the earth."

There is a difference between the time of Tribulation and the day of the wrath of God. The opening of the sixth seal will take place between the Tribulation and the great day of the wrath of God. In Revelation 6:17, the Bible says, *"For the great day of their wrath has come, and who can stand?"*

Why do I say that the opening of the sixth seal will take place between these two events? Jesus mentions this in Matthew 24:29: *"Immediately after the distress of those days "'the sun will be darkened, and the moon will not give its light; the stars will fall from the sky, and the heavenly bodies will be shaken.'"* He describes the events just as they are pictured in Revelation 6, by the opening of the sixth seal. We can also read what Peter wrote in Acts 2:19–20:

"I will show wonders in the heaven above and signs on the earth below, blood and fire and billows of smoke. The sun will be turned to darkness and the moon to blood before the coming of the great and glorious day of the Lord."

Jesus said that the events of the sixth seal will take place immediately after the Tribulation, and Peter said that they would take place immediately before the day of God's wrath.

Let us compare in more detail at what Jesus said in Matthew 24 and what is written in Revelation 6. Matthew 24:29: *"Immediately after the distress of those days "'the sun will be darkened, and the moon will not give its light;"* Revelation 6:12: *"The sun turned black like sackcloth made of goat hair, the whole moon turned blood red."* Matthew 24 continues: *"the stars will fall from the sky,"* and in Revelation 6:13 we read, *"and the stars in the sky fell to earth, as late figs drop from a fig tree when shaken by a strong wind."* In Matthew 24 we read, *"and the heavenly bodies will be shaken."'* And Revelation 6 says, *"The sky receded like a scroll, rolling up, and every mountain and island was removed from its place."*

Furthermore, we read in Matthew 24:29, *"At that time the sign of the Son of Man will appear in the sky, and all the nations of the earth will mourn. They will see the Son of Man coming on the clouds of the sky, with power and great glory."* Later, in Matthew 24:38–39, we read:

"For in the days before the flood, people were eating and drinking, marrying and giving in marriage, up to the day Noah entered the ark; and they knew nothing about what would happen until the flood came and took them all away. That is how it will be at the coming of the Son of Man."

I have made this a very detailed comparison in order to show that the events connected with the opening of the sixth seal were already announced by Jesus in Matthew 24.

What does all of this mean? The time of the Tribulation is the time when the antichrist will be in power, and will fight against those of God's children who will still be on earth, in order to annihilate them. God will not allow this. Then something will happen on earth. God

Himself will orchestrate the events that will take place. The Bible calls this the day of God's wrath.

The other great event that takes place during the time of the sixth seal, before God's judgment will come upon the earth, is the sealing of the one hundred and forty-four thousand Israelites. This sealing will protect these Israelites from the apocalyptical judgment to come. The Overcomers, the bride of Christ, are no longer on earth. The people who have come out of the Tribulation will also have been Raptured. Notice: before the judgment will come over the earth, and the day of God's wrath begins, God will take His own away from this earth, and those who remain, the one hundred and forty-four Israelites, will be sealed, so that the judgment cannot affect them. God's people can and will experience persecution by those who were sent by Satan, but they will never have to endure the wrath of God.

THE SEVENTH SEAL

The wrath of God is ushered in with the seventh seal. The introduction to this seal comes with half an hour of total silence in heaven. There are seven angels standing before God. They are subordinate to God, and they have many other angels under their command. God works under this concept of authority. We can find a similar chain of command in the Old Testament, especially in the organization of David's kingdom.

Each of the seven angels was given a trumpet to announce the judgments upon the people, the antichrist, and the devil. We notice that another angel, who had a golden censer, came and stood at the altar and prepared God's judgment. Then something will happen! There will be peals of thunder, rumblings, flashes of lightning and an earthquake, and as the Bible says, the declaration of God's judgments. Then the seven angels will fulfill their assignments.

The Bible says in Revelation 8:7, *"The first angel sounded his trumpet, and there came hail and fire mixed with blood, and it was hurled down on the earth. A third of the earth was burned up, a third of the trees were burned up, and all the green grass was burned up."*

This is very similar to what we read in Exodus 9:22–25, when God sent Moses to Egypt and the plagues came upon the Egyptians. These plagues were a judgment sent by God over Egypt. The plagues came only upon the Egyptians. The Israelites were not affected. The Bible tells us when the first angel sounds his trumpet, a third of the vegetation on earth will be destroyed. This is difficult to imagine.

The second angel will sound his trumpet. In Revelation 8:8-9, we read about a huge mountain, which was ablaze and was thrown into the sea. A third of the sea turned into blood, a third of the living creatures in the sea died, and a third of the ships were destroyed. We must realize that this judgment is not directed upon the sea, but against the people. The judgments of God pertain to people.

In 1937, a huge object with a diameter of two to three kilometers was detected in the universe. It was named Hermes, and there was fear it could plunge to earth. However, it turned away and disappeared. Scientists tell us that if such an object would fall on earth, there would be inconceivable destruction. Entire continents could vanish. The Bible tells us that such an object will come. It will land in the sea and cause a devastating catastrophe, a tidal wave, the size of which has never been seen before. We can imagine the kind of devastating catastrophe that will be! Just think of the tsunamis in Sri Lanka, Indonesia and Japan, which caused the death of many thousands of people, and of all the destruction they left behind. A large part of the shipping industry will be destroyed, and world trade will be devastated. The fishing industry will suffer immense damage in many countries.

Then the third angel sounds his trumpet, and we read in Revelation 8:10-11:

> "The third angel sounded his trumpet, and a great star, blazing like a torch, fell from the sky on a third of the rivers and on the springs of water—the name of the star is Wormwood. A third of the waters turned bitter, and many people died from the waters that had become bitter."

Will this be a burning meteor? A third of the world's fresh water will be polluted. The Bible says the waters turned bitter, many people died from drinking these waters, and there will be no more fresh water.

The Bible continues to tell us that the fourth trumpet will sound. This will affect the sun, moon and stars; a third of them will turn dark. The Bible states that after John saw this, he heard an eagle flying in the midst. It is not necessary to speculate about who this eagle is, but it is important to know that he called out in a loud voice, "Woe! Woe! Woe to the inhabitants of the earth" (Revelation 8:13).

Someone may ask, "Would a God of love do such things?" Up to the beginning of chapter 8, God *allowed* things to happen, but now He is dealing with the inhabitants of earth. He had exercised patience and love, and in return, people ignored, rejected and willingly turned away from Him. They became more and more hardened against Him. His righteousness demands justice.

After the warning from the eagle, the fifth trumpet was sounded. The fifth trumpet signals the first woe. The Bible says something very interesting about this: *"And I saw a star that had fallen from the sky to the earth. The star was given the key to the shaft of the Abyss"* (Revelation 9:1).

The Bible often speaks of stars. In Revelation, the Bible calls the leaders of the churches stars. Sometimes angels are referred to as stars in the Bible—good angels as well as evil ones. It speaks of stars as an example of meteors, and it speaks of stars in heaven's firmament. The context of its use will usually reveal to what the word "star" refers. In these verses, it speaks of a star that had fallen to the earth, and had been given a key. It was someone who was able to take action. Who was that? He opened the mouth of the abyss. This must be a high-ranking angel sent from God. The Abyss is the place where thousands of fallen angels are now held in captivity. An important leader is among them. When the first woe comes, this abyss will be opened, and the Bible tells us that smoke will rise out of it, and a plague will come over the earth, over all those who have not been sealed.

People will be stung like the sting of a scorpion; that is, the effect will be like that of a scorpion's sting. Apparently, there are few things on earth as painful as the sting of a scorpion. Soldiers have reported that men stung by scorpions have rolled around on the ground, frothing at their mouths. The stings are not deadly, but terribly painful. The Bible tells us that this plague, caused by the demons come out of the abyss, will come over the people on the earth. People will suffer for five months. They will want to die, but will not be able. Why is the Bible telling us all this? In Luke 21:36, Jesus says, *"Be always on the watch, and pray that you may be able to escape all that is about to happen, and that you may be able to stand before the Son of Man."*

Do you know what the Bible is trying to reveal so plainly to us in Revelation? It is to tell Christians from what they have been saved, delivered, set free and protected, and how God offers salvation to all through Jesus.

God wants to remind us to watch and to stay away from sin, to be ready and to completely submit to Him. He wants to show us something else; namely, that there are still many people who do not know Him and who will experience this catastrophe, unless they accept Jesus Christ and His salvation. God also wants to remind the church to go forth, and to preach the gospel unto all nations.

THE SIXTH TRUMPET

The Euphrates River is two-thousand and eight hundred kilometers long and it ran through the Garden of Eden. The first onslaught of the devil upon God's creation, man, and upon the earth, which God had entrusted man to oversee, occurred in this area. The first murder and the first great rebellion against God, brought on by Nimrod when he tried to build a giant tower to reach up to heaven, also occurred here. Since then, man has erected many and much higher buildings, but the idea behind the building of the tower was to be able to reach God. It meant a revolt against God. In this area of the Euphrates, the first world ruler built his kingdom, a human kingdom.

God's word tells us that the four bound angels were to be released. These were evil angels, because only evil angels are bound and imprisoned. In Jude 6 and in 2 Peter chapter 2, we read that God has kept angels who rebelled against Him bound with chains. Without a doubt, these are four of the devil's princes. Shortly after their release, they will have amassed a large military force. Their influence upon people without God is phenomenal. We must realize that this will not take tens of years. This shows us a little of the power of demonic spirits upon people, and that the nature of the demonic spirits is to cause destruction and corruption. Only the grace and goodness of God has kept them until this time from doing what they would like to do. Satan's nature is that of a thief and a murderer, and his angels have his characteristics.

We see a huge army. John tells us the number he heard—two hundred million. We have to realize that, at that time, there were not even two hundred million people living on the earth. The trust John had in His Lord was so great that he knew whatever God said was true, and would happen. I can well imagine that the critics in his day, after reading this, would have said, "John, such a thing is impossible!"

Let us look at Revelation 9:17 and 19:

"The horses and riders I saw in my vision looked like this: Their breastplates were fiery red, dark blue, and yellow as sulfur. The heads of the horses resembled the heads of lions, and out of their mouths came fire, smoke and sulfur...The power of the horses was in their mouths and in their tails; for their tails were like snakes, having heads with which they inflict injury."

Here we see that weapons of destruction will be used. We have to remember that John describes these pictures according to the things he knows, and with which he is familiar. There probably will not be real horses. Could they be tanks or mobile rockets? Whatever they are, the results will be horrible and terrible. The Bible says that fire, smoke and sulfur will be the elements of destruction used here. The results show us that this will not be a conventional war. The Bible tells us that, within a relatively short time, a third of mankind will be killed by these three plagues: fire, smoke and sulfur.

A short time before this, when the fourth scroll was opened, John had seen that a fourth of mankind was killed at the time of the disagreement with the antichrist. We must try to visualize how our earth will appear at that time: a fourth of mankind will be killed at the opening of the fourth seal, the bride of Jesus will be Raptured, the great multitude that will have come out of the Tribulation will have been taken up to God, there will be those who have died during the catastrophes, and now a third of the remaining population will be killed. Yes, the earth's population will rapidly decrease!

The Bible goes on to say, after John saw this picture, that the second woe will occur. *"The rest of mankind that were not killed by these plagues still did not repent"* (Revelation 9:20). This shows something about the wickedness of the human heart. Mankind will still not turn to God. They will see the obvious evidence of God's judgment and will experience God's reality like at no other time, but they will remain hard, just like Pharaoh, who had experienced the many wonders of God. His heart remained hardened because he did not want to humble himself before God. Man is proud. He does not want to humble himself, nor acknowledge the Lordship of God.

John talks about four things that will be prevalent during that time: murders, occultism, sexual immorality, and thefts. The things mentioned here will not just be present at that time; these things have been firmly rooted in man's nature. Let us examine each one individually. Murder—we find this everywhere. It is used for political gain. Murder is used as a weapon, and bombings and the killing of people are justified. This is only one aspect of it. Let us think of the unaccountable murders of children occurring daily through abortions. Do not ever think that man will not reap what he sows!

The second thing mentioned is occultism and magic arts, and the addiction to drugs. Occultism and magic arts already existed in the Middle Ages, and even in the Old Testament. They have always been present in all countries. However, today we find that occultism and magic arts have made their way right into the upper classes of society, right into the highest intelligentsia. There are even universities with professorships for these subjects. Our generation accepts this as a matter of fact. The media portrays these practices as normal.

Sexual immorality is the next offence. This has also existed throughout history. However, who could have imagined that laws would be changed to legalize same sex marriages and permit pornography on television? They try to tell us that this is all part of the Arts, because it has been publicized in a movie, in a picture, in a song or in a book.

Thefts are mentioned. Of course this does not only refer to bank robbery, home invasions or street muggings, but pertains to every kind of theft, even the most modern example of illegal downloading of movies or music. Unfortunately, the attitude prevails: as long as I can get away with something, it's okay.

Notice, we already live in a time where all of these things are accepted as matter of fact. We have turned away from God's commandments, and people themselves have decided what is right and what is wrong. We try to justify ourselves and say, "If there is a God, why does He not intervene and bring an end to everything?" Why does He not do so? Because God is patient and He does not want mankind to be lost. He wants to give us time and opportunity to repent!

Stop and think! What would have happened to us if God had judged us immediately? Would many of us have been saved? Every time when a person comes to Jesus we must admit, "Lord, how wonderful it is that you are patient and have not yet said it is enough!"

THE ANGEL WITH THE SCROLL

What we read in Revelation 10 will probably take place before the last, the seventh, trumpet is sounded. It is not important to define the exact moment when this will happen. Revelation was not given to us so that we could start speculating. It was given to show us what God would eventually do and what would happen on earth, so that we would concentrate on Jesus Christ and on His Word.

Here we have a mighty angel coming down from heaven. Personally, I believe this mighty angel is Jesus. I believe this because this angel was robed in a cloud and arrives in a cloud. Whenever we read in the Bible about heavenly clouds appearing, it always refers to God. We saw this in Exodus 9. The Lord appeared in a cloud; as the Israelites fled Egypt and did not know which way to go, God led them as a cloud by day and a pillar of fire by night. When Jesus ascended into heaven, He was taken up by a cloud. In Revelation 1:7, we read, *"He is coming with the clouds."* According to Revelation 4, the rainbow belongs to God and to His throne. The Bible tells us that the angel who appears in chapter 10 has a rainbow above his head, and his face is like the sun. Let us go back to the first chapter in Revelation, verse 16, which refers to Jesus, saying, *"His face was like the sun shining in all its brilliance."* In the Bible, this expression always refers either to God or to Jesus. When Jesus was on the transfiguration mountain, the Word of God tells us in Matthew 17:2, *"His face shone like the sun, and his clothes became as white as the light."* Here again we find the same expression which always refers to God or Jesus. The Bible goes on to say that the angel's legs were *"like fiery pillars."* Revelation 2:15 says about Jesus: *"His feet were like bronze glowing in a furnace."*

This angel had a little open scroll in his hand, and he placed one foot on the earth and the other on the sea. What is in this scroll? In chapter 5 we read about a scroll that was sealed. The only book ever mentioned in the Bible was the sealed scroll. We also saw that there was no one worthy to open the seven seals except Jesus, the Lamb. Since Revelation 5, one seal after another was opened. By now, it is understandable that the formerly sealed scroll, containing the title deeds of the earth, had to be open at this time. Jesus, the only one who was worthy to open the scroll, now assumes legal ownership of the earth.

In the Old Testament, the assumption of ownership was a symbolic act, signified by putting a foot on something. Deuteronomy 11:24 says, *"Every place where you set your foot will be yours,"* and in Joshua 1:3 we read, *"I will give you every place where you set your foot, as I promised Moses."*

After all the seals had been opened, Jesus assumed ownership of the earth. Some may ask, "Doesn't the earth belong to God? Why is Jesus just taking ownership of it now?" It is true that God created the earth and everything in it, and on the basis of creation, the earth belongs to Him. However, after God created the earth and after He created man, He entrusted the earth into the care of man. This is not only important as far as what we read in Revelation, but also as far as the conditions we see around us today. In Genesis 1:26–28, the Bible says, *"Then God said, 'Let us make mankind in our image, in our likeness, so that they may rule over the fish in the sea and the birds in the sky, over the livestock and all the wild animals, and over all the creatures that move along the ground.'"* So God created mankind in his own image, in the image of God he created them; male and female he created them. God blessed them and said to them, *"Be fruitful and increase in number; fill the earth and subdue it. Rule over the fish in the sea and the birds in the sky and over every living creature that moves on the ground."*

God gave dominion over the earth to man. Then a great tragedy occurred through the sinning of man. The right to lease, which God had given man, went over to the devil in a legitimate manner. Therefore, man is no longer the ruler over the earth, but Satan is. God had to accept this because He gave man sovereign authority over the earth, but man sold it to the devil. In Luke 4:5–6, when Jesus is tempted by the devil, it says:

> *"The devil led him up to a high place and showed him in an instant all the kingdoms of the world. And he said to him, 'I will give you all their authority and splendor; it has been given to me, and I can give it to anyone I want to.'"*

Someone may say, but the devil is a liar, he has lied from the very beginning. That is true; but remember, had he lied here, it would not have been a temptation for Jesus. The devil had received power over the earth, and then he wanted to persuade Jesus to fall down and worship him because he craves to be worshiped. Jesus refused to do so. After hundreds of years, the moment had now arrived when Jesus took over the rightful sovereignty of the earth, the sovereignty the devil had offered Him. It was not because He bowed down to Satan, but because He fulfilled the plan of redemption. He was able to open the seals, and He was victorious, not only for Himself, but also for man who had transferred this position to the devil. Can we now understand why our earth is such a mess? Please do not say, as many Christians do, that everything is happening just as God wants. That is not true! God does not want war and sorrow. He does not want poverty and suffering. He also does not want the murder of many children who have not yet been born. The reason for this is that man gave the enemy the right to rule over this earth and mankind. That is why we have so much misery on this earth.

Jesus became eligible to nullify this lease document by completing the plan of redemption, and therefore taking back control of the earth. What man lost will now be transferred back. After John saw this angel, who stood with this little scroll in his hand, he had no doubts as to what he should do. He heard the seven thunders, and understood what they were saying. He wanted to write it down, but God told him not to because people did not need to know this. Then John heard this angel give an oath. He said that there would be no more delay. One could say, "*It is time!*"

We get the impression that Jesus is very pleased with the proclamation, and that is why He promised the living God there would be no more delay. The time had come, and there would not be any more delays. What time? It is the time when the mystery of God will be revealed, the time in which the devil was allowed to rule over the earth will be over, and there will be no more delays. Here on earth it usually appears that the stronger one succeeds and remains victorious, whether he is just or unjust. As long as the devil is in charge, and people listen to him, it will be so. It will not remain like this; it will stop. Not only will it stop, but God's justice will take over.

The mystery of God's plan, His dealings with people since the fall, and His plan to reclaim the kingdom and to give it to the saints will then be revealed. God will return the dominion of the earth to the one who always should have owned it—mankind. Mankind, who will obey God, who will submit to God, and who will not say like Adam and Eve did, that they did not want God to rule over them. Who is this? It is a person who has accepted the salvation God has completed through Jesus Christ. These persons will then receive dominion over the earth. God's initial plan will be fulfilled with all who obey Him and all who did not rebel against Him.

Subsequently, something interesting takes place. John received the order to eat the scroll. It tasted good, but it turned sour in his stomach. What is the symbolic meaning of this? Jesus will return to the earth after he has opened the seals. He will symbolically take over the ownership of the earth, and will give the deed of ownership to man, man who has overcome by the blood of the Lamb, of whom John is a representative. With this, the rightful ownership will be returned. What did Jesus say in His sermon? Blessed are the meek, for they will inherit the earth. Now this will actually happen. This will be a wonderful and terrific experience for all Overcomers, to receive this privilege from God. There will also be a bitter side to this, in that the same people, the redeemed, who have received this ownership of the world, will fight with Jesus in order to complete this transaction. The people will have to be judged, and this will happen at the opening of the seals, in which the redeemed will partake. This will be very painful; it will be the bitter side of this. However, God's righteousness is at work here.

THE TEMPLE AND THE TWO WITNESSES

Revelation 11:1—14

John received this vision around 95 A.D., while he was on the island of Patmos. The temple in Jerusalem, known to Jesus, had been destroyed and ravaged approximately twenty-five years earlier by Titus and the Roman Legions. The temple being discussed here in Revelation 11 must still be built. It is not the original temple which was in Jerusalem. Daniel 9:27 says that the antichrist will make a treaty with Israel, and it appears that because of this treaty there will be an opportunity for the building of this temple. We read in this verse, *"He will confirm a covenant with many for one 'seven.' In the middle of the 'seven' he will put an end to sacrifice and offering. And at the temple he will set up an abomination that causes desolation, until the end that is decreed is poured out on him."*

Whenever God measures something, whether for weight or as it is here with a reed, He wants to measure and examine the spiritual state of a nation or of an individual. Here, it is about the spiritual state of the Nation of Israel, who once again has instituted sacrificial offerings, but the Jews will not yet have accepted Jesus as Messiah. During this time, they will hear a powerful testimony about Jesus, but as a nation, they will not have accepted Him as Messiah. The Bible tells us that during this time, for a period of forty-two months, Jerusalem will be surrounded by Gentiles. The outer court will be trampled for forty-two months. I believe that here we see the actual fulfillment of the words written in Luke 21, where Jesus says that Jerusalem will be trampled by Gentiles, until the times of the Gentiles will be fulfilled. The 1967 conquest of Jerusalem was already a giant step toward the direction of this prophecy; however, it will not happen until the time is fulfilled, and in the time between, Israel will be trampled upon by Gentiles.

The Bible speaks here about two witnesses who were to work in the city of Jerusalem. I would like to point out the time of their work. God's word says that their work will end with the second woe or with the sixth trumpet. If their work is supposed to end with the second woe, and the Bible tells us that the woe will last forty-two months, then we can ascertain that these two witnesses will appear in Jerusalem at the same time the seals are opened. They will appear during the time when many events will be occurring in the entire world. They will have a very definite, interesting and prominent duty to fulfill.

Who are these two? One of them is probably the prophet, Elijah. Let us look at Malachi 4:5–6, the last verses in the Old Testament:

"See, I will send you the prophet Elijah before that great and dreadful day of the Lord comes. He will turn the hearts of the fathers to their children, and the hearts of the children to their fathers: or else I will come and strike the land with a curse."

Someone could say the Bible meant John the Baptist; didn't Jesus Himself say that it was him? And do we not read that John the Baptist was supposed to be the predicted Elijah?

It is not unusual for a Biblical prophecy to pertain to two events. Let us look at what the Bible says in Matthew 17: 10–11: *"The disciples asked him, 'Why then do the teachers of the law say that Elijah must come first?' Jesus replied, 'To be sure, Elijah comes and will restore all things.'"* He said this after John the Baptist was already dead! Furthermore, He said, *"But I tell you, Elijah has already come, and they did not recognize him, but have done to him everything they wished."* Does Jesus not say that John on the one hand was Elijah, but that Elijah will still come, just as it had been stated in Malachi 3? It is astounding that Elijah was the prophet who never died. He was literally carried up to heaven in a chariot of fire. Who will be the other witness who is mentioned here? Personally, I believe it will be Moses. The miracles that these two will perform are identical to the ones Moses performed when he appeared before Pharaoh.

Let us look at how Moses left this earth. Moses was only able to see the Promised Land from a mountain, and then he died. It is interesting that the Bible says that his grave was never found. The Bible merely states that God buried him. The New Testament reveals an important clue in Jude 9: *"But even the archangel Michael, when he was disputing with the devil about the body of Moses."* Where else was the body of a person taken from this earth up to God? It appears that after Moses died, God took the body up to heaven. Remember what happened when Jesus took three of His disciples up to the Mount of Transfiguration. Who came to Him to discuss His departure from earth? The Bible tells us it was Moses and Elijah.

They will appear during the reign of the antichrist, when there will be great confusion on this earth. What will be their mission, and why will they have come? At first, they will expose the antichrist, draw attention to Jesus Christ, and will witness about Him. Besides this, they will be here as prophets who will preach about judgment. They will connect all of the events happening on earth with God's judgment. They will exhort the Jews to repent and to turn to God.

The Bible says they will have great opposition. We can easily imagine this if we place ourselves in their situation. The antichrist will have appeared and will have been accepted by a large part of the world as the person who has the solution to all of the world's problems. Even the nation of Israel will make a treaty with him. His achievements will be remarkable as he tries to find ways to overcome the chaos present here on earth. At that time, both of these men, who will be in complete opposition to the antichrist, will appear. They will do this in a manner which will make them famous throughout the world. There will be a great conflict between them and the antichrist. During that time, there will be many things happening in the world. It is interesting to note that the antichrist will not be able to kill these two men. He will not be allowed to touch them for forty-two months. Whoever wants or tries to kill them will instead be killed by them. Fire will come out of their mouths, and those who try to hurt them will be devoured by them; this is how they must die. They will have the same power Elijah had, to pray to shut up the sky so that it will not rain. They will have power to strike the earth with every kind of plague. Just as Pharaoh continued to harden his heart instead of turning to God and humbling himself before Him, we read in the Bible that, in spite of this, people did not repent.

The two prophets will testify about Jesus, and will show the world that the antichrist is an imposter. They will be against him, and will perform many amazing things on the earth. During this time, the antichrist will try his utmost to kill them, but he will not succeed. Many will ignore them; however, some will find salvation because of them. Even though they will be in Jerusalem and will perform their duties there, the whole world will be aware of them and will be influenced by them.

Then something will happen whereby the world will think that a victory has taken place. It will appear that the antichrist possesses the most power. After forty-two months, the antichrist will suddenly succeed and will be able to kill them. He will take credit for their deaths. He will receive congratulatory messages from everywhere throughout the world because these two, who had caused such unrest, were killed. There will be great joy and celebration throughout the world. There will be celebrations, and people will give each other gifts, just as we give gifts in memory of Jesus' coming to earth. The idea is to prove to the world that the antichrist is the most powerful.

The bodies of these two will be put on public display in Jerusalem. This will be transmitted throughout the world via satellite, and will prove to all they are dead. While the celebrations are still going on and the TV cameras are still focused on them, something extraordinary will happen. They will stand on their feet and before the eyes of the world will be taken up into heaven. A great terror will strike the world.

At the same time, there will be a great earthquake in Jerusalem. A tenth of the city will collapse, and seven thousand people will be killed. All of this will be directly transmitted via satellite throughout the entire world. The Bible says that survivors were terrified. The second woe has passed. Let us look at what the Word of God says in Revelation 9:21: *"Nor did they repent of their murders, their magic arts, their sexual immorality or their thefts."* The word of God will melt the hearts of some people, while others, like Pharaoh, will harden their hearts. To those who open their hearts, the gospel of Jesus Christ is like perfume; to those who close their hearts it causes hardness. Whenever we hear the gospel, and God's Spirit speaks to our hearts, and we shut Him out, we will not remain the same; our hearts will become harder. The more we shut out the gospel, the harder our hearts will become. God can perform signs and miracles, dead may rise, but if our hearts have been hardened, these things will have no effect upon us. Those who have accepted the gospel will experience God's grace and mercy in continuous new ways. It is terrifying to know that people can have such clear evidence, and yet remain hard. It shows just how far people have come when they have turned away from God. That is why they are ready for judgment.

The events associated with the seven trumpets are again confirmed in the second part of Revelation. In Revelation 15:5–16:21, they are described as seven bowls of wrath. The discerning reader will realize that the same events have been described.

THE SEVENTH TRUMPET OF THE SEVENTH SEAL

Revelation 11:14—15, 19

These few verses summarize the most horrible event that will come upon people. Specific details are found in chapters 15, 16 and 17, which describe the seven bowls of God's wrath. Let us discuss them in order.

The Bible says, *"The kingdom of the world has become the kingdom of our Lord and of his Christ."* (Revelation 11:15b)

Throughout the Old Testament, God's people always had a great longing to have an earthly kingdom where there would be peace and well-being. In many ways, God Himself had prophesied such a kingdom through His prophets. In connection with this, the prophets spoke about God's servant, who first had to suffer, before this kingdom would come. Israel was so fixated on such a kingdom that it totally ignored the message about the servant who was going to die. That is why even the disciples expected Jesus to establish such a kingdom while He was on earth. How disappointed they were when this did not occur. That is why they asked in Acts 1:6, *"Lord, are you at this time going to restore the kingdom to Israel?"* He answered them, *"It is not for you to know the times or dates the Father has set by his own authority. But you will receive power when the Holy Spirit comes on you; and you will be my witnesses"* (Acts 1:6–7).

In the New Testament it is about belonging to a spiritual kingdom. Jesus taught about this as He began to preach, *"Repent and believe the good news!"* (Mark 1:15) Insofar as a person trusts in God and submits to Him now, so will he then have a part in that earthly kingdom. The moment will arrive when the earthly kingdom will be established under the authority of Jesus Christ.

God's Word says in Revelation 10:7, *"...the mystery of God will be accomplished, just as he announced to his servants the prophets."* This will happen when the seventh angel sounds his trumpet. The mystery of God will be accomplished. God's plan will be fulfilled! Jesus will establish His kingdom on this earth.

When Jesus comes to power on this earth, all other forms of government man had tried to establish will cease to exist. God's people have prayed for such a long time, and still pray today, *"Your kingdom come"* (Matthew 6:10). God's kingdom will come! If people would only understand God's plan, and how God wants to involve us in His plan! God will only accept those in His kingdom who were voluntarily born again into His kingdom, because they believed in His salvation and submitted to His authority.

The seventh trumpet includes something else. The Biblical account states that the time had come for rewarding God's servants and the prophets. 2 Corinthians 5:10 says, *"For we must all appear before the judgment seat of Christ, so that each of us may receive what is due us for the things done while in the body, whether good or bad."* About whom is the Bible speaking? The Bible is speaking about those who are saved, the children of God. 1 Corinthians 3 speaks about this. Our lives, as Christians, will one day be examined and tested by going through God's fire. The question will not be whether we shall be saved. The question about salvation is decided by a personal decision in response to Jesus' substitutionary death on Golgotha. Then Jesus will judge how we lived as Christians. God's Word is very clear about this: God will not judge according to the magnitude of a deed, but He will judge according to the motivation of one's heart. In the refining process of God's fire, large deeds could burn up, whereas so-called small deeds will be untarnished. It will depend upon our inner motivation and our convictions. If we do something just to be noticed by people, we can rest assured this deed will burn up before God. That is why the Bible tells us that everything we do, whether in words or deeds, should be done in the name of Jesus. The Bible does not mean we should go around saying, "I am doing this in the name of Jesus." It is not according to a spoken formula, but according to the state of our heart.

I believe that this judgment will be a great moment of joy for many people. Many will say, "But Lord, when did I do this for you?" And Jesus will answer, "When you did this for the least of mine, you did it with true love toward me." I also believe there will be many who will be crying. The tears will be wiped away in the New Jerusalem, but I am not certain about here. We will remember all the opportunities God gave us to change and become more like Jesus, but if we have continued to hold on to our selfishness, we must face up to the results of our actions. That is why the Bible says, and it is not just speaking to non-believers, *"Today, if you hear his voice, do not harden your hearts!"* (Hebrews 3:15)

It is wonderful to be saved, but the Bible teaches that God wants us to grow and develop. He wants to bring us to the point where our deeds will be acceptable to Him. My wish for all of us is that we would examine our lives in the light of salvation through Jesus, and whether we are born again. We should also examine ourselves as to how much we have changed and have become more like-minded with Jesus, so that our deeds will endure before God.

The Bible says the dead will also be judged during the time of the seventh trumpet. The seventh trumpet will bring everything to the final conclusion. The Bible states that the dead will rise during this time. In John 5:28–29, we read:

> *"Do not be amazed at this, for a time is coming when all who are in their graves will hear his voice and come out—those who have done what is good will rise to live, and those who have done what is evil will rise to be condemned."*

God's Word tells us that there will be approximately one-thousand years between the resurrection of the righteous and the resurrection of the unrighteous. Just as God has judged His children according to their deeds, so will He judge the deeds of those who have not accepted Christ as their Savior.

We also read that during the seventh trumpet the temple of heaven will be opened. In connection to this, two things impress me. According to Revelation 15, it will be necessary that the temple in heaven be opened so that the seven angels with the seven bowls of God's wrath are able to come out, and the final judgment can come upon this earth. We also see something else. The Ark of the Covenant was in sight. Even though God's judgment will come upon this sinful earth, He always reminds us that He will keep His covenant. If God has made a covenant with us, and we with Him, he will never, never break it. We can break it, but God will never! If we could only fully comprehend the love, the grace and mercy of our Father! I believe we would serve Him with greater submission and would appreciate Him more. Only the person who rejects this love and mercy will be condemned. We must remind ourselves that love is the strongest force in existence, just as hatred is the weakest. There is no greater power than love, and that is our God, our Father. Whoever rejects this love will be condemned.

God does not make it simple for a person to be lost. Some have tried to break away from Him, but His love, His power, was there, and in the end they could not do so. Today they are very thankful for God's love. Only those who reject this love will be lost. God has a marvelous plan for every person. What can we do to present God's message in a way in which God's plan can be better understood? God is good, and He will remain good. It is only due to His goodness and love that our earth still exists. If God were anything like us, the earth and everything on it would be long gone. His mercy toward all people is immeasurable. There is one thing we must realize—God does not give up on people, even if we have given up on them. God tells us in His Word what will happen to this world; not because He has decided and determined a specific percentage of saved and unsaved people. This warning is another appeal to us. He is clearly showing us what will happen to those who ignore His love.

THE HARVEST OF THE EARTH

REVELATION 14:14–20

W hat kind of harvest is this? Let us read Matthew 24:29–31:

> "Immediately after the distress of those days 'the sun will be
> darkened, and the moon will not give its light; the stars will fall
> from the sky, and the heavenly bodies will be shaken.' Then will
> appear the sign of the Son of Man in heaven. And then all the
> peoples of the earth will mourn when they see the Son of Man
> coming on the clouds of heaven, with power and great glory.
> And he will send his angels with a loud trumpet call, and they
> will gather his elect from the four winds, from one end of the
> heavens to the other."

This is the harvest, a time of happiness for God. We can read
about a similar event in Matthew 13, and again we want God's Word to
speak to us. In this passage, Jesus is speaking about a man who sowed
good seed, and then his enemy came and sowed weeds among the good
seed. The owner's servants noticed that the good and bad seeds
sprouted. The servants asked whether they should go and pull up the
weeds. The Bible says in Matthew 13:30, "Let both grow together until
the harvest. At that time I will tell the harvesters: First collect the weeds

and tie them in bundles to be burned; then gather the wheat and bring it into my barn." We continue to read in verses 37–39, *"He answered, 'The one who sowed the good seed is the Son of Man. The field is the world, and the good seed stands for the people of the kingdom. The weeds are the people of the evil one, and the enemy who sows them is the devil. The harvest is the end of the age, and the harvesters are angels.'"*

The harvest in which Jesus will be involved is the "taking up" of the living Christians on earth after the great Tribulation and before the horrible day of the wrath of God. These Christians went through the Tribulation. Let us notice something: since the beginning of mankind, until this moment, there has been "good and bad seed" existing side by side on this earth. Now the moment has arrived when things will change. How much grief had the children of evil caused the believers? The moment will come when there will be a harvest and a separation of the two. It will happen during this time. While the antichrist is raging and fuming and has issued the decree that Christians should be persecuted, God will say, "This is the end!" Jesus Christ, Himself, will be involved in the Rapture of those who went through the Tribulation and who will be allowed to come to Him.

Let us try to imagine what the earth will look like after the great Tribulation, which will last only during the reign of the antichrist. After the time of Tribulation, the day of the wrath of God will commence. All Christians will have been removed from the earth. Who will remain? It will be the antichrist with his prophet, the devil with his angels, who had been hurled to this earth, and an unbelieving population. This will be a time of darkness as never before. This will be the moment when the extent of God's judgment will come over the earth. The Bible calls this the great winepress of God's wrath. This day will end with the battle of Armageddon. This will be discussed in more detail in chapter 19. The most horrifying event ever seen on earth is about to happen.

Who Will Be Present at the Rapture of the Bride?

As I have already mentioned, I believe that a Rapture will occur before the time of the great Tribulation, and I believe that there will be a

Rapture during the time of the Tribulation. Both groups of believers are children of God, but will not have identical rank or responsibilities in heaven.

Most Christians do not realize there is still so much to gain and so much to lose upon becoming a believer. We read in Philippians 3:13–14, *"Brothers and sisters, I do not consider myself yet to have taken hold of it. But one thing I do: Forgetting what is behind and straining toward what is ahead, I press on toward the goal to win the prize for which God has called me heavenward in Christ Jesus."* What is this goal? It is the prize of victory for your heavenly destiny.

Paul is not talking about salvation or being born again. He already was saved and born again. He was not thinking about the new life one receives upon accepting Christ. Paul had experienced this, and remained steadfast in this new life. He went so far as to say nothing could separate him from the love of God which is found in Jesus Christ—not death, nor demons, nor trouble nor hardships nor anything else. He said, *"I know whom I have believed, and am convinced that he is able to guard what I have entrusted to him until that day"* (2 Timothy 1:12). Paul was confident about his salvation, about his new birth, and about being a child of God. He wrote to the churches, *"Rejoice in the Lord that you are saved."* He also wrote, *"You have been made righteous by faith in Christ Jesus."* To the Philippians he wrote in Philippians 1, *"He who started a work will bring it to completion."* Even though he was so confident about being a child of God, about his salvation, and that nothing could separate him from the love of God, he was still pressing onward toward something that he had not yet received. He said that a Christian who has become a believer and has been born again should strive to attain the prize of victory. Many people assume that once they are saved, they have fulfilled God's purpose in their lives. All that is left is to never reject Christ. The word of God tells us that even saved people have the right to attain a prize. Paul tells us in Philippians 3:11 what this prize is. The prize of victory is that he wants to attain the "out" resurrection from the dead. That is what is written in the original text.

Paul was convinced about the resurrection, and he wrote to the Corinthians and the Thessalonians that we shall be resurrected from the dead. Yet he mentioned that this goal, this prize of victory, led to the possibility to be part of the resurrection in the first Rapture, to be among those who will sit upon thrones with Christ, and to reign with Christ. Every Christian can attain this prize. We cannot add anything to our salvation or to our becoming children of God; however, we can and must do something if we wish to attain this prize. God's Word tells us that we have to make every effort and surrender ourselves to do so. Now we realize why throughout the ages God has exhorted believers to be prepared, because He could come any day.

God knew right from the beginning that many generations of believers would not experience His return during their lifetime. Yet, through His Word and the Holy Spirit, He exhorted all believers throughout the generations to live as if Christ's return would be today. Why? The belief they had when they left this earth will count when the Rapture occurs. All those, who had the same belief when they died as the people will have when Jesus returns, will be resurrected and will be Raptured. They will be a part of the multitude the Bible calls the Overcomers, the First Fruit, or the Bride. These will sit with Jesus on the throne and will reign with Him. The way we live will determine this.

In the Bible, there are definite characteristics people must have in order to be part of the Rapture. This pertains to all who want to be part of the Rapture, whether they have already died or are still alive when this event happens. They will be believers, born again people—like Enoch, an example for this Rapture— who walk with God. If we keep this is mind, we must realize that more is required than just to be born again. It involves our whole life.

What Does It Mean to Walk With God?

It means to be together constantly day and night. How would we live our lives if we could actually see Jesus beside us? Have you ever thought about this? What kind of thoughts and fantasies would we have? How would we speak if Jesus would always be with us? How would we act with Jesus beside us? What places would we visit, and which ones would we avoid if Jesus were always with us? What literature would we read, and what would we not? What kind of things would we watch if God would always be visible in our lives? What kind of friends would we have? What would be our life? What plans would we make and complete? Enoch walked with God. This does not mean he walked five kilometers with God. Enoch lived his live together with God, day and night, in his thoughts, his actions, in everything. The people who will be part of the Rapture before the Tribulation will be people who have walked with God. Do we understand why the Bible tells us in Hebrews 11:5 that Enoch's testimony was that he pleased God, before he was taken away from this earth?

Secondly, the people who will be part of this Rapture will be prayer warriors. Jesus said in Luke 21:36, *"Watch and pray that you may be able to escape all that is about to happen."* In the Old Testament, Elijah is an example for the Rapture before the Tribulation. God's word says that Elijah was a person with the same feelings as all of us. As a child, I always admired the prophets. I thought they were super heroes— people who came from different beings than we did, until one day I found this verse in the Bible: Elijah was a person with the same feelings as we. Do we not all picture men and women of the Bible as so much better than we are? Elijah was a man of prayer. The people who will take part in the Rapture before the Tribulation will be people who pray. How is your prayer life?

The Bible goes on to say they will be Overcomers. When we read the seven letters to the churches, we notice that each ends with the same thought—to him who overcomes I will give him the right to sit with me on my throne, etc. What do we have to overcome? The Bible gives us an answer in 1 John 2:13: we are to *"overcome the evil one."* In 1 John 5:4, it says, *"For everyone born of God, overcomes the world."* We also read in Romans 8:37, if we are in Christ then we shall overcome fear, persecution, Tribulation and the desires of our flesh. Overcomers are people who, though faced with all of these obstacles of life, will have learned to live in victory with Jesus.

The Bible continues to say that the children of God, who will be present at the Rapture before the Tribulation, are virgins. This does not mean unmarried women. Men are also included. This is an expression used by the Bible to explain and describe a way of life. It speaks about being separated from the world and about practical holiness. I am well aware that this word, holiness, is not welcomed by everyone. The Bible says in Matthew 5:8, *"Blessed are the pure of heart, for they will see God."* We also read in 1 Thessalonians 4:3, *"It is God's will that you should be sanctified,"* and in Hebrews 12:14, the Bible says, *"Make every effort to live in peace with all men and to be holy; without holiness no one will see the Lord."*

It is sad to say worldliness has crept into many lives and into many churches. The Bible teaches that love toward the world breeds a lukewarm Christianity. *"Don't you know that friendship with the world is hatred toward God?"* (James 4:4) In regards to this, God makes a very strong point. He says that people who befriend the world are spiritual prostitutes and adulterers. God's word states this. We live in a time when—and this is very painful to me as a leader of a church—worldliness in church is accepted as normal. We live in a time when if we lovingly correct someone who is living in such a situation, that person will feel insulted, become angry and, sad to say, will go around the corner and find a church who will gladly accept and welcome him.

To lower the standard of God's holiness in a church should never become an issue. Holiness should be esteemed more. We should separate and be different, should think differently, speak differently, act differently and never make a compromise. Many movie theaters, discos and nightclubs are not suitable places for Christians. God views the drive for materialism as idol worship. The endeavor to become rich by compromising your inner life will cause you to miss the goal. The Bible says it is God's will to be holy.

Let us never forget that sin nailed Jesus to the cross. It was sin that made it necessary for God to sacrifice His son. This should cause every Christian to make a huge detour around sin. We should never think, as some do, that it does not matter if we sin. We are weak, and can always go back to God and say that we are sorry and ask for His forgiveness. This is true. God, in His goodness and grace, says that we are to forgive someone who comes to us, seven times seventy times a day. He will forgive each of us, but if we continue to sin, we do not understand what holiness means. Do not expect to be in the group of Overcomers without living holy lives. The Bible speaks about a group who will be saved as if going through fire, but they will suffer some consequences.

The people in the group who will be Raptured before the Tribulation will follow the Lamb wherever He goes. This means obedience. Where does the Lamb go in our life? How does God show us where He is going in our life? He begins to speak to us through the Word of God and through our conscience. There are people who simply do not want to obey Jesus. They are in the church, and may even have a ministry in the church, but there is no obedience. The people who follow the Lamb obey the great desire of Jesus to preach the gospel. Have you noticed that the willingness to preach the gospel of peace belongs to God's spiritual weapons for the believers? This is God's greatest desire. He said that the message of the gospel must be preached throughout the entire world.

There are people in churches from every area of the world who have been saved. Why? He wants them to return to their world, to continue to preach the gospel, and to follow the Lamb, wherever He goes. Are we obedient?

In connection with this, the Bible says that such people are trustworthy; there is no deceit in them and the words coming out of their mouths are true. The Bible continues to say that the people who will take part in the Rapture before the Tribulation will have oil in their lamps. Oil is the symbol of the Holy Ghost. When the Bible says they have oil in their lamps, it does not speak of only one experience with the Holy Ghost. It means to have the characteristics of the Holy Ghost.

The people who are a part of this Rapture—whether they died earlier or are still alive—all longed to see the return of Jesus. Let us look at 2 Timothy 4:7–8:

> "I have fought the good fight, I have finished the race, I have kept the faith. Now there is in store for me the crown of righteousness, which the Lord, the righteous Judge, will award to me on that day—and not only to me, but also to all who have longed for his appearing."

Let me give each of us a simple test for our lives. How do we react to the idea of Jesus' return? Do we long for His return, or do we say, as many do, "I would actually prefer if He would wait a little longer?" I know this from my own life when I always hoped, "Lord, don't come too soon!" Looking back today, I am so thankful that He did not come at that time. There were no major reasons or serious mistakes, but there was no joy at the thought of His return. Only if we have made Jesus the most important thing in our hearts will we have true joy at the thought of His return. If there is anything we value more than Jesus, we will notice that the thought, "Come soon Lord Jesus," will cause no happiness. I would like to advise each one to change his attitude, whether it relates to a person, a thing, business, career or a hobby. Let Jesus become the dearest thing in your life. People who will be in that Rapture whether young or old, are people who already pray: "Lord Jesus, come soon!"

We are able to judge the time by the signs the Bible gives us. People who belong to the Overcomers live in a daily dependency on God. They are not self-assured, but totally depend on God.

Ask yourself, if Jesus came today, would you go with Him? Notice these people do not make just one decision and then forget about it. They focus their entire life on Jesus. This is God's wish for each person. Does every Christian do this? There are so many who are indifferent as to how they live. Occasionally, they make another start with God and clean out their lives, but soon return to their old way of living. They do not follow the Lamb; they do not value their lives.

THE BOWLS OF WRATH

REVELATION 15:1–8, 16:1–21

Revelation 14 ends with the harvest and the gathering of the grapes. These two events are completely separated from one another. The harvest is the gathering of the believers during the time of the antichrist's reign, as we have discussed. Revelation 14 also speaks about the gathering of the grapes; this is described in chapter 15. Those who remain behind on this earth end up in God's winepress. This was mentioned earlier when we discussed the Day of God's Wrath.

This judgment will begin with a certain event in heaven. This is described in verses 5–8. Heaven is preparing for the events that will occur on earth. Not one of us can understand or imagine the immensity of the coming terror. From the seven bowls of wrath, a succession of judgments will come upon the people who did not want to know anything about God, upon the devil, and upon the antichrist and his prophet. Seven angels will be called and they will be prepared. They will receive seven bowls filled with the wrath of God. In John's first vision, he saw seven angels blowing trumpets while these judgments were fulfilled. Now he is seeing something entirely different concerning the same events.

Do not ever forget that the God of love and mercy is also a holy God. The Bible tells us that at this time He is not filled with anger as we would be, but because of His righteousness, He must sentence the people who resisted Him with a righteous judgment. The Bible says in the gospels, *"Whoever believes in the Son has eternal life, but whoever rejects the Son will not see life, for God's wrath remains on him"* (John 3:36).

The time has come when God's judgment will fall upon the antichrist, his prophet and over all people who have rejected Him. During the judgment, God's temple will be filled with the Glory of the Lord. The revelation of the Glory of God is a spice for life for some, and for others it is a judgment for death.

The first angel will pour out his bowl. What will happen? The Bible says that ugly, painful sores broke out on all people on this earth—not just a few, not on just one city, but all people will be affected by these sores. The Bible mentions these will be terrible and very painful. Just as in the time of Moses, when a similar plague came over the people, doctors will not be able to find a remedy. It seems that one plague will not be over before the next one appears. This first plague will still be going on when the next angel empties his bowl.

The Bible says when the second angel pours out his bowl, the sea (two thirds of our earth is covered with water) will be turned into blood like that of a dead man. I am not mistaken when I say that the seas will become a useless mass. Can we begin to imagine what the result of this will be? Just think of the oil spill in the Gulf of Mexico in 2010! This will cause the death of sea creatures. The shipping and fishing industries will be bankrupt. What will happen to the wonderful, fresh breezes that come from the sea?

The third angel poured out his bowl on the rivers and springs of water, and they became blood. How much blood has been spilled upon this earth? How much blood is still being spilled today? God seems to ignore this, but He takes account of abortions, whether legal or illegal. This is a righteous punishment.

The fourth angel will pour out his bowl, and this will affect the sun. There will be a heat wave as never seen before. People will be scorched by the heat. We cannot imagine the intensity of this. The rivers will be turned into blood, the seas will be useless and there will be no life, just decay, and unbearable heat on the earth.

The fifth angel will pour out his bowl, and there will be unbelievable darkness upon the earth. This is symbolic of the spiritual darkness in which people will be.

When the sixth angel pours out his bowl, evil spirits will go forth throughout the earth, specifically three main demons. Their assignment will be to amass the armies of the world to one spot, which will be the Euphrates River. The river will have dried up for this purpose.

We read about this in Zechariah 4 and 5. There will be an earthquake. Jesus will return to this earth, and will be accepted as the Messiah by approximately one third of the Israelites. They will recognize the One whom they had killed, and they will know that He is Jesus, their Messiah. This will happen! This is written in the Bible, and there is no other book as dependable as the Bible!

We live in a time in which preparations are being made for these events. We live in a time in which the coming of Jesus is very imminent. How does this affect each one of us? These events I have mentioned actually do not concern God's children, thank the Lord, but they do concern many people who are not yet children of God. What does Jesus say? He states that His biggest desire, before His return, is that the gospel of the kingdom of God should and must be preached to all nations, before the coming of the terrible and great day of the Wrath of God.

It is not by chance, that in Matthew 25, Jesus talks about two pictures connected with His return—two pictures that we should definitely take seriously. He speaks about the ten virgins, five wise and five foolish saying, *"Therefore keep watch, because you do not know the day or the hour"* (Matthew 25:13). Do not allow anyone who thinks they know the day and the hour of His coming to mislead you. God's word also says you are not like those who sleep. For the children of God, Jesus will not come like a thief in the night. Due to the events happening in our time, it is evident that His return is close at hand. Therefore, keep watch! Jesus also said that we should use our talents to work for Him and to proclaim the gospel.

BABYLON, THE PROSTITUTE ON THE BEAST

Revelation 17:1—18

What is described in Revelation 17 will probably happen while one of the bowls is being poured out. It was the responsibility of one of the seven angels to show these things to John. This chapter speaks about the punishment for the false religion. Revelation 18 speaks about the punishment for the culture and business world. These two are closely related. However, when we study chapter 18, we will find significant differences. In chapter 17, John sees this woman whom the Bible calls a prostitute with a title written on her forehead. Her name was Mystery, Babylon, the Great Mother of Prostitutes.

It is interesting to note that John was led into a desert in order to see her. When the bride of Jesus was shown to him, he was taken to a mountaintop. Now that it concerns the spiritual prostitute, he was taken to a desert. Why such a terrible name as prostitute? This is probably the worst name one can call a woman. In the Bible, Israel and the New Testament church of Jesus are always referred to as wife, as woman or even as virgin. That is how God sees the church. Spiritual prostitution occurs when there is false worship, idol worship and the introduction of rituals. God is no longer in the place that is rightfully His. Other things have replaced His position.

Forgiveness is available for all who have sinned. God's Word tells us that Christians can commit sin, and they can be forgiven. However, those who are involved in idol worship, even modern idol worship, and have rejected God are in great danger. Idol worship, spiritual prostitution and adultery are horrible. There are many examples about spiritual prostitution and adultery in the Bible. God discusses this in Jeremiah 3, Hosea 1, and Revelation 2.

Revelation 17 tells us that John was astonished when he saw the picture of this woman. The actual phrase used is that he was filled with horror. I noticed that John was not surprised when he saw the Beast or the development of the political power on earth. He was not surprised about many other things but now, when he saw this woman, this prostitute, he was filled with horror. It is obvious this woman represents a people involved in a doctrine of idol worship. Whenever Israel was unfaithful to God, it was because of idol worship, and whenever there was idol worship, witchcraft was always involved.

Near the beginning of the Bible, we read about the birth of idol worship. It happened immediately after the flood, a few generations after Noah, in Babel. Genesis 10 informs us about this. Nimrod, a descendant of Noah, built the tower of Babel. Not only were the languages thrown into total confusion, but idol worship was born.

What was the purpose of this construction? Was it not the idea to build something to exalt themselves, and to tell God, "We do not need you anymore; we will not listen to you anymore!"

A very informative book by Alexander Hislop, *The Two Babylons*, states that while Nimrod was the political leader at that time, his wife Semiramis was the spiritual leader. A son was born to this woman, and she insisted that he had been conceived by a ray of the sun. She then decided that this son was the descendant from the woman, concerning the prophecy to Eve, found in Genesis 3:15. Supposedly this son was attacked and killed by a wild boar. She cried and fasted for forty days, and then her son supposedly came back to life. This is when the worship of a mother and her little child began. She was elevated to the position of Queen of Heaven, and became a priestess. They began to worship this mother and the little child she held in her arms.

Abraham lived during this time, and this is likely the reason why he received the message from God to leave the home of his father, to leave his homeland and this religion. God took him out of this situation because He wanted to start something new and to create a new nation with him. Many of Nimrod's descendants accepted the type and manner of worship that started in Babel. In the course of time, some of Abraham's descendants also adhered to this kind of worship. Over time and distance, names of these false deities have been changed: in Assyria it was Ichthal and Tammuz, in Egypt it was Osiris, in Phoenicia it was Asterod and Baal, or Tammuz, in Greece it was Aphrodite and Eros, and in Rome it was Venus and Amor. This form of worship became similar throughout many thousands of years. There were always the two figures, a mother and son. Added to this were forty days of fasting. There were special offerings of cakes made to the Queen of Heaven, and at the end of the fast there would be a huge celebration.

The prophets spoke against this cult. In Jeremiah 44, we read that God spoke to His people clearly, and admonished Israel about their idol worship and their turning away from Him. The people turned against the prophet, and in Jeremiah 44:17 and 19 we read:

> "We will certainly do everything we said we would: We will burn incense to the Queen of Heaven and will pour out drink offerings to her just as we and our ancestors, our kings and our officials did in the towns of Judah and in the streets of Jerusalem…The women added, 'When we burned incense to the Queen of Heaven and poured out drink offerings to her, did not our husbands know that we were making cakes impressed with her image and pouring out drink offerings to her?'"

The core of this idolatry was to bring offerings to the Queen of Heaven.

Ezekiel 8 also speaks about this kind of worship. The prophet was shown the great atrocities occurring amongst God's children. In Ezekiel 8:13–14, we read how God's Spirit spoke to him: "*Again, he*

said, 'You will see them doing things that are even more detestable.'
Then he brought me to the entrance of the north gate of the house of the
LORD, and I saw women sitting there, mourning the god Tammuz."
This was many years after the building of the tower of Babel, and they
still had the time of fasting and the time of mourning for this child. It
was idol worship, birthed in Babel. This idolatry made its way to Rome.
There, Caesar became the Pontifex Maximos, the high priest of this
idolatry.

When spiritual life had departed from the early general Christian
church and the idea was born to forcefully win people for Christianity,
it was decided to introduce this line of idolatry into Christianity. They
started to worship and pray to a mother and son, and they instituted
forty days of fasting followed by a great feast. God had ordained a
special contribution for Mary in the church, but it was not until
hundreds of years later that they made her a special mother figure with
her son, to whom one could pray. Under Christian names and titles,
they introduced the cult of praying to pictures and saints.

Now do we understand why John was horrified when he saw this
woman? Even if he could have imagined many things, one thing he
could not have imagined was that such idolatry could make its way
inside Christianity. John saw this woman riding on a beast. The beast
was the symbol for world empires, Assyrian, Egyptian, New-
Babylonian, Med-Persian, and Greek. All of these had passed away.
John lived during the Roman Empire, to be followed by the future
empire of the antichrist, which will commence when the antichrist
arrives.

The woman John saw appeared to be wealthy. She was dressed in
fine clothes and adorned with jewels. She rode on the earthly powers
and ruled over them. John was acquainted with the church of Jesus. He
knew that it was poor, scorned, despised and persecuted. What he now
saw was a religious system in Christian clothing, which had been
accepted, had power, displayed authority and would participate in the
affairs of the world rulers. He was horrified. Jesus had never spoken
about this—this was news to him.

Then he saw that she was drunk. It actually says that she was
constantly drunk with the blood of the saints. During the time in which
John lived, it was Rome and the Jews who did not accept Christ, and

they persecuted the Christians and killed them. However, this was a religious Christian system John saw, which was responsible for spilling the blood of the disciples of Jesus.

The Bible describes the sudden collapse of this system. It will happen through the very ones who were involved and had worked in harmony with it. They will suddenly destroy it. In Revelation 18, we read that God destroyed the city of Babylon. God will destroy the cultural and commercial developments throughout the world. In chapter 19, God Himself will overthrow the beast and the false prophet. In chapter 17, it is not God, but people who will destroy this system of idolatry. The same people, who lived in and with it, will carry out God's judgment. John was impressed as he wrote his letters and gave much advice. He closed his first letter with the words, *"Dear children, keep yourselves from idols"* (1 John 5:21). Do we understand why? We must keep away from this system. Remember, Jesus Christ is the only Mediator between God and man, and *no one* comes to the Father except through Christ. Remember what Jesus said, *"I am the way, the truth and the life"* (John 14:6). Remember that it is Jesus Christ, through His Holy Spirit, who must work, can work and will work to bring renewal in our hearts.

THE FALL
OF BABYLON

R evelation 18 has much in common with chapter 17. Some would conclude that they discuss the same matters. Babylon is discussed in both chapters. In chapter 17, Babylon is called Mystery, while in chapter 18 it is the Great City of Babylon.

Careful reading of these chapters will reveal there is a very noticeable difference. In Revelation 17, the religious, disloyal system against God in Babylon will be judged by man, namely by the antichrist. In chapter 18, the Great City Babylon will be judged by God. In chapter 17, we get the impression that the judgment over "Mystery" Babylon will not be sudden, but will happen over time. In chapter 18, God's judgment over the city will happen instantaneously. We often read, "in one hour," suddenly, this city will be gone.

What is the meaning of this Babylon in Revelation 18? The expression, Great City of Babylon, is used throughout the chapter, and one could get the impression that this city would have to be rebuilt in order for it to be destroyed again. The expectations are that this city on the Euphrates River by the Persian Gulf will be rebuilt. It seems logical that the revenues from oil production will add to the wealth of this city. There is another train of thought that the Great City of Babylon does not represent a city such as New York, but represents the commercial and cultural systems which have influenced and determined the outcome of commerce throughout all centuries. We will look at the Great City of Babylon as the commercial system, which, together with the Mystery Babylon, has determined and ruled the world throughout centuries.

Why would God's judgment come upon Babylon, upon this system? Revelation 18 explains this. In Revelation 18:5, we read: *"...for her sins are piled up to heaven, and God has remembered her crimes."* It often seems as if only the bad succeed. Those who remain on the right path are always the losers. Have we often thought and heard others say that the wicked win? Justice is not worth it. Honesty only causes disadvantages. Only those without scruples get somewhere, and only the schemers and the deceitful will get ahead. Many business people have accepted this as the norm in order to get ahead. God notices these things, and by Him, sin remains sin.

In the Old Testament, there is a word applicable not only for a personal life but also for a whole nation and for the entire global commercial system. The Bible says, *"Your sins will find you out"* (Numbers 32:23). Do not be deceived. We may be able to hide and cover up our sin for a long time, and we may be able to continue sinning in secret, thinking that no one sees us. However, God will make certain that our sins will find us out, unless they have been forgiven through the blood of Jesus Christ! Otherwise, the moment will come when our sins will be revealed—it will be at the end. At the end, when God's people will be gone, God will judge injustice and sin. Revelation 18:7 states another reason, she gave herself much glory and luxury, *"In her heart she boasts, I sit as queen; I am not a widow, and I will never mourn."*

In this system there is no God, no Lord to serve, no Savior, no Holy Spirit, only selfishness, self-glorification and self-promotion with callous ambition and only one goal, to become wealthy. James talks about this in James 5, starting in the first verse:

> *"Now listen, you rich people, weep and wail because of the misery that is coming on you. Your wealth has rotted, and moths have eaten your clothes. Your gold and silver are corroded. Their corrosion will testify against you and eat your*

flesh like fire. You have hoarded wealth in the last days. Look! The wages you failed to pay the workers who mowed your fields are crying out against you. The cries of the harvesters have reached the ears of the Lord Almighty." (Do not forget, this also includes factory workers and other employees.) *"You have lived on earth in luxury and self-indulgence. You have fattened yourselves in the day of slaughter. You have condemned and murdered the innocent one, who was not opposing you. Be patient, then, brothers and sisters, until the Lord's coming. See how the farmer waits for the land to yield its valuable crop, patiently waiting for the autumn and spring rains. You too, be patient and stand firm, because the Lord's coming is near."*

God says He is taking account of these things, and if we in our work accept this unfair situation, God Himself will judge this self-righteous, self-centered system.

Sad to say, there are many people who are personally just like this system. They strive only toward material possessions, even if it is at the cost of their salvation and spiritual well-being. They are a part of this system, and the Bible says that one day it will be judged. It does not depend on the millions you may have saved; it depends on the attitude that motivates your life.

In Revelation 18:12–13, we find another reason why God will judge this system. These verses mention twenty-seven reasons, starting with gold and ending with bodies and souls of people. There is so much mentioned, all under the direction and control of this system, and all originating from egotism. Notice, this includes the buying of groceries, luxury items, furniture, industry, specialty items, medication, the stock market, and even the slave trade. Today, humans are more knowledgeable than ever before. We have had so many experiences no other generation has had. There have been so many inventions, and we are still in the midst of new developments no one would have ever imagined. We have more information available to us than ever before. In relatively few hours, we are able to travel from one continent to another. All of this has not made us better people, instead we have become less compassionate. Are we perhaps more horrible and more ungodly than previous generations? We would be shocked if we saw and knew what is really happening in our world! God takes account of all these things.

It so comforting for us to know that this Jesus, who considers us so special, died for us. He said because we became His children, He would protect us, lead us and guide us in the midst of an evil world. I find this to be powerful! We should be more aware that we are, as far as our spirituality is concerned, in a wrong environment. However, our shepherd will guide us through.

Revelation 18:24, gives us yet another reason why God will send this judgment upon this city and upon this system: *"In her was found the blood of the prophets and of the saints, and of all who have been killed on the earth."* This cannot refer to only one city which has been rebuilt and then destroyed in the end times. In that city it would be impossible to spill the blood of all the saints. This system, which has existed for hundreds and even thousands of years, is responsible for the murder and shedding of the blood of all the prophets and saints. The Bible states something else: God judges not only one's actions, but also what is in the heart, the motivation (Mark 7:17–23).

We should thank God for the laws of our country that protect us. These laws were instituted mostly by people who feared God. Without these laws there would be chaos, and our lives would be different. There are many people with evil in their hearts. God will judge not only their actions, but also their evil hearts.

We also find an appeal to God's people for holy living. In Revelation 18:4, it is written: *"Come out of her, my people, so that you will not share in her sins, so that you will not receive any of her plagues."* The Bible does not say, and I do not want anyone to misunderstand me, that we should leave this world. Paul said that we cannot clean up this world. Jesus prayed, They are not of the world, even as I am not of it (John 17:16). In Romans 12:2, Paul wrote, *"Do not conform to the pattern of this world, but be transformed by the renewing of your mind."*

I believe that the Bible means that we should change our attitude, not only about the ungodly religious system, but also about the commercial and ungodly thinking that is taking place in our time. This is not about a geographical change. It is about an inner change in our thinking, our opinions, our decisions, and in the goals and focus for our life. That is what counts. Change, leave this behind. Those who do not change will receive the same punishment as this city.

I believe that Paul was talking about this when he wrote in 2 Corinthians 6:14–18:

"Do not be yoked together with unbelievers. For what do righteousness and wickedness have in common? Or what fellowship can light have with darkness? What harmony is there between Christ and Belial? Or what does a believer have in common with an unbeliever? What agreement is there between the temple of God and idols? For we are the temple of the living God, as God has said: 'I will live with them and walk among them and I will be their God and they will be my people. Therefore, Come out from them and be separate, says the Lord. Touch no unclean thing, and I will receive you. I will be a Father to you, and you will be my sons and daughters, says the Lord Almighty.'"

Many people believe they can do both. On the one hand, serve God, and on the other hand, go along with the world and be part of it. They live as if they are testing God. They are probably the most miserable people. Young and older people will never be more miserable than when with one hand they hang on to Jesus and with the other hand on to the world. This causes the greatest inner turmoil. Let go of the world and worldly thinking, and take hold of Jesus, His word, and His thinking and lead your life accordingly. God said to come out from among them so that you will not be guilty of the same punishment.

We cannot change the world system. Jesus did not call us to change the world. He called us to *"Go into all the world and preach the gospel to all creation. And Whoever believes and is baptized will be saved"* (Mark 16:15–16). They will be saved from this system. This is the mission of the Church.

We should live as closely as possible to the Lord, walk with Him and adjust our life according to His plan and will. We do not have to avenge God to defend Him. He will do that in a fair manner, as only He can. He is so good, so patient and so loving. He always gives us another chance to change, to turn away from sin and to come to Him. However, one day it will be too late, and then He will judge the world as well as the system that rules this world.

THE WEDDING
OF THE LAMB

In this passage there are many Hallelujahs. The first one is for the downfall of the Prostitute of Babylon. It is a shout of joy and thankfulness that God has finally acted. The second Hallelujah is for the destruction of the City of Babylon and this unjust system, which has been controlling the world for hundreds of years.

The third Hallelujah is in exultation of our Lord, Jesus Christ. Jesus Christ defeated the enemy on the cross; He broke Satan's power; He overcame him. Jesus arose and is seated at the right hand of the Father as Conqueror. As far as this world is concerned, the devil will still be conducting his business. Do you remember how John cried when no one was found worthy to open the book with the seven seals? It was the Deed of the World, and no one was found to be worthy except the Lamb who was slain. The book of Revelation describes what will happen when these seals will be broken. This will be the moment when Jesus assumes control of the world, when He will be honored as King of Kings. While this is happening, a large multitude will be shouting, "Hallelujah, Amen!" These people did not just begin to learn to worship in heaven; they practiced this while living on earth. God loves it when His people praise and worship. He inhabits the praises of His people.

The fourth Hallelujah is in Revelation 19:5. It is the answer to a voice from the throne. This voice is inviting people to praise and worship God, to honor and to extol Him because the wedding of the Lamb has arrived. We get the impression that next to Salvation on Golgotha, this wedding is the most important event to God and His Son.

The bridegroom is introduced first. Who is he? The bridegroom is Jesus. In 2 Corinthians 11:2, Paul wrote that Jesus was the bridegroom of a pure, godly virgin. We find a similar picture in Ephesians 5:23–32, which is the well-known scripture often read at weddings, where it compares Christ and the Church to the bride and groom. Here we are discussing Jesus' wedding. In the first thirteen verses of Matthew 22, we read about the wedding banquet. People had been invited, but what did the invited guests do? They ignored the invitation and went about their daily business. They did not commit something terribly bad. It is no sin to work on your farm; it is no sin to take care of your family, but all these things were more important to them than the wedding. When the actual wedding took place, the call went out to invite all who wished to come. The invited guests had to remain outside.

In order to have a wedding, one must have a bride. The bride is not Israel; the bride is what the Bible calls the first fruit, the Overcomers, the virgin. We notice something very interesting in the Bible. This bride is dressed in fine, bright and clean linen. The dress she is wearing stands for the righteous acts of the saints. The bride of Jesus wears two dresses. This may be news to some, or it may not have been noticed. The first dress she wears is the dress of the righteousness of Jesus, which covers up her nakedness. She received this dress when she became saved and was born again. This dress is important in order to be saved, but the bride of Jesus wears a second dress on top of the first one, and that dress is for the righteous acts of the saints.

The dress of Christ's righteousness is a gift. Whoever does not accept it as a gift will not receive it. Paul wrote, the gift of God is everlasting life. We cannot earn salvation from sin; Jesus earned this when He died on the cross. Every person should be wearing this dress. There is nothing easier than to put on this dress because it is free. All one has to give for it is the dress of self-righteousness, which the Bible calls a dress of rags. This should be discarded and exchanged for the dress that is offered to us—the dress of Christ's righteousness. Each person who wears this is saved from his debt of sin.

The Bible is speaking of a second dress, the dress of the righteous acts of the saints. This dress is different. The first dress was a gift, but the second must be earned. This dress is our reward for our obedience and our devotion to Jesus, and as a result of our inner change to become more like Jesus. While Jesus was responsible for attaining the dress of His righteousness, and we can have it as a gift, we are responsible for obtaining our own dress for the righteousness of the acts of the saints.

In 2 Corinthians 5:10, the Bible says that all of us must appear before the judgment seat of Christ, where we shall find out whether or not we shall receive this dress. In 1 Corinthians 3:11–16, the Bible gives us another picture of this. We shall pass through fire, and the fire will test the quality of each man's work and reveal what will survive. In both passages, the Bible tells us that our works and our way of life will determine how this dress will look. The same chapter tells us that even though some people have a Christian life, their deeds as children of God will be burned up when they have to go through this test by fire. The Bible tells us that they will be saved, but they will receive only the dress of Christ's righteousness, nothing more.

The Bible also tells us when some Christians pass through the fire, their lives will be found to be like gold, silver and costly stones. It is very important how each of us lives as a Christian. It is of utmost importance how obedient we are to Jesus and His Word, how submissive we are to Jesus. This will determine whether we shall be brides. Jesus fulfilled the plan of Salvation with one aim, and that is to have each one of us as bride. That is why He surrendered Himself; it is His greatest desire! It does make a difference whether we live a pure and holy life. It makes a huge difference whether we accept God's Word as it is written, and whether we obey Him.

The Bible speaks of a wedding. There is very little said about it, except that it has now arrived and there is much jubilation in heaven, such as never before. It is apparent that it has been a long time in coming, and now finally the moment has arrived. Both the bridegroom and the bride have long waited for this moment. This picture is very much connected with the customs of wedding feasts of that time. It was customary that the bride and groom were engaged to each other at a very early age. The Bible speaks of Mary and Joseph being engaged to one another. Being engaged did not mean living together! Being engaged meant preparing and waiting for the wedding. Preparations for a wedding were more elaborate than they are today. Finally, it was time for the wedding and the great feast. This feast will come for Jesus and His bride. The order in the Bible is somewhat different from the one we practice today. For us, the bride is the most important figure in a wedding, and everything is about her. However, the Bible first introduces the bridegroom, and then the bride.

We discussed the seven letters to the churches. What was the theme of these letters? Was it about being saved or condemned? No, the letters are about whether or not to be a bride. Read them with this in mind: whether you will be His bride, whether you will stand by His side and whether you will sit on His throne where only the bride can be. This is what the letters are about. They want to motivate us to be brides.

THE BATTLE OF ARMAGEDDON

The battle of Armageddon is the moment when Jesus Christ personally intervenes in the history of mankind on earth. This will take place after the wedding of the Lamb about which we read in Jude 14: *"See, the Lord is coming with thousands upon thousands of his holy ones to judge everyone, and to convict all of them of all the ungodly acts they have committed in their ungodliness, and of all the defiant words ungodly sinners have spoken against him."*

The last war has often been predicted in the Bible, not only in Revelation. Let us look at several of these scriptures, in order to get a better understanding and a better connection about what is written here. We have read in Revelation 11:15, *"The seventh angel sounded his trumpet, and there were loud voices in heaven, which said: 'The kingdom of the world has become the kingdom of our Lord and of his Messiah, and he will reign for ever and ever.'"*

Here is an announcement of the same event. In Revelation 14:14–20 we read:

> *"I looked, and there before me was a white cloud, and seated on the cloud was one like a son of man with a crown of gold on his head and a sharp sickle in his hand. Then another angel came*

out of the temple and called in a loud voice to him who was sitting on the cloud, 'Take your sickle and reap, because the time to reap has come, for the harvest of the earth is ripe.' So he who was seated on the cloud swung his sickle over the earth, and the earth was harvested."

The word of God continues by telling about the harvest:

"Another angel came out of the temple in heaven, and he too had a sharp sickle. Still another angel, who had charge of the fire, came from the altar and called in a loud voice to him who had the sharp sickle, 'Take your sharp sickle and gather the clusters of grapes from the earth's vine, because its grapes are ripe.' The angel swung his sickle on the earth, gathered its grapes and threw them into the great winepress of God's wrath. They were trampled in the winepress outside the city, and blood flowed out of the press, rising as high as the horses' bridles for a distance of 1,600 stadia."

In Revelation 16:12–16, we again read about this. It is reported that as the sixth angel poured out his bowl on the great River Euphrates, three evil spirits looking like frogs came out of the mouth of the dragon, out of the mouth of the beast, and out of the mouth of the false prophet. We continue to read: *"They are the spirits of demons performing miraculous signs, and they go out to the kings of the whole world to gather them for the battle on the great day of God Almighty."* This is the same event.

In the Old Testament, in Isaiah 63:1–6, we read:

"Who is this coming from Edom, from Bozrah, with his garments stained crimson? Who is this, robed in splendor, striding forward in the greatness of his strength? 'It is I, proclaiming victory, mighty to save.' Why are your garments red, like those of one treading the winepress? 'I have trodden the winepress alone; from the nations no one was with me. I trampled them in my anger and trod them down in my wrath; their blood spattered my garments, and I stained all my

clothing. It was for me the day of vengeance; the year for me to redeem had come. I looked, but there was no one to help, I was appalled that no one gave support; so my own arm achieved salvation for me, and my own wrath sustained me. I trampled the nations in my anger; in my wrath I made them drunk and poured their blood on the ground.'"

We find here the same description about the trampling of the grapes, as in Revelation 16, only in the language of the Old Testament, as the prophet had seen it. We read about the same event in Joel 3:12–13: *"Let the nations be roused; let them advance into the Valley of Jehoshaphat, for there I will sit to judge all the nations on every side. Swing the sickle, for the harvest is ripe. Come, trample the grapes, for the winepress is full and the vats overflow—so great is their wickedness."*

Let us pay attention to how the Old Testament goes on to describe this event in Joel 3:14–17"

"Multitudes, multitudes in the valley of decision! For the day of the LORD is near in the valley of decision. The sun and moon will be darkened, and the stars no longer shine. The LORD will roar from Zion and thunder from Jerusalem; the earth and the heavens will tremble. But the LORD will be a refuge for his people, a stronghold for the people of Israel. 'Then you will know that I, the LORD your God, dwell in Zion, my holy hill. Jerusalem will be holy; never again will foreigners invade her.'"

It should absolutely astound us that God had already prophesied this, thousands of years earlier. Many hundred years later, He gives John this vision on the island of Patmos. John does not think of this prophecy, and yet the same things were seen.

In Zechariah 14:1–5, we read:

"A day of the LORD is coming, Jerusalem, when your possessions will be plundered and divided up within your very walls. I will gather all the nations to Jerusalem to fight against it; the city will be captured, the houses ransacked, and the women raped. Half of the city will go into exile, but the rest of

*the people will not be taken from the city. Then the LORD will
go out and fight against those nations, as he fights on a day of
battle. On that day his feet will stand on the Mount of Olives,
east of Jerusalem, and the Mount of Olives will be split in two
from east to west, forming a great valley, with half of the
mountain moving north and half moving south. You will flee by
my mountain valley, for it will extend to Azel. You will flee as
you fled from the earthquake in the days of Uzziah king of
Judah. Then the LORD my God will come, and all the holy ones
with him."*

We have prophecy from the Old Testament, we have the words in
Revelation, and we could read Daniel 2, 7, 9, and 11, as well as Ezekiel
37 and 38, and we will find the same event described in each. What is
actually happening here? What does God's Word tell us? What is the
battle of Armageddon?

During the time of the Tribulation, Israel will make a treaty with
the antichrist. Then, Israel will break this treaty with him and the
federation of ten nations. From that moment, the antichrist will not
only be against Christians, but also against Israel. We have seen that
those Christians who did not accept the sign of the beast will be taken
away from the earth. The result will be that the antichrist will suddenly
not have any Christians to persecute, but will now also go against
Israel! Then something remarkable will happen. The nations of the
world, from north, south, east and west will prepare to go to the
Middle East to fight against Israel. This little spot on earth, this tiny
nation, will have the entire world's attention upon itself. They will
wage war to finally eradicate it.

The Bible tells us that the nations of the world will come together.
How is this possible? According to war strategy, it would not be
necessary to have so many armies go against Israel. What will happen?
We read about it in Revelation 16. Demon spirits will be instrumental
in making this happen. Demons will have definite powers over the
people. In 2 Thessalonians 2:11, we read, *"For this reason God sends
them a powerful delusion so that they will believe the lie."*

Enemy forces will surround Israel, and this nation will be certain
that its end has come. Israel has only one opportunity left, and that is

to call upon God for help. The battle will begin, and the Bible tells us in Zechariah there will be attacks on Jerusalem. I do not think this will last many days. Jerusalem will be occupied. Half of the city will be ransacked, and the other half destroyed. Finally, the Nation of Israel will call upon God! Then it will occur! Jesus will visibly come to the earth. We have read it; His feet will stand on the Mount of Olives. The angels had proclaimed that this Jesus would come again in the same manner as He went to heaven. He will return, not just in Spirit as during the time of the Church, nor will He return, as some claim, in the minds of Christians. He will return as He was, and will stand upon this earth. With Him will come the believers who had been Raptured and those who had been resurrected.

The Jews will then see the One they had crucified, the One they had rejected, and the One to whom they had said, "May His blood come over us and our children." How true this will have become! Then they will see Him, and Israel will experience salvation. The people alive at that time will accept Jesus as their Savior, and will acknowledge Him as their Messiah. They will realize their error and will say, "Lord, forgive us for rejecting you." They will accept Him, and He will fight for them and He will triumph! The antichrist, the false prophet, and the diabolic powers of the earth will also see Him. He was the one who no longer existed for them, the One whom they had declared as nothing and against whose descendants they had fought. Now, He will suddenly stand before them. The Bible tells us that He will defeat them with a sword in His mouth. Remember what happened to the soldiers in the garden when Jesus was captured? Jesus asked them, *"Who is it you want?"* They answered, *"Jesus of Nazareth."* He then answered them, *"I am he, let these men go."* As He said this, they drew back and fell to the ground. What power the words of Jesus have! What a powerful moment that will be when He returns as a majestic king.

Jesus will see all the armies who are fighting against Israel, who are in fact fighting against Him. There will be the beast, the antichrist and all the kings, or leaders, of the earth. There will be the false prophet. We read in Revelation 13 that the people cheered after the antichrist's fatal wound healed. Who resembles the beast? This was his high point, and at that time he was able to convince many who had still been skeptical about him. Now, he will meet the one who is much stronger than he was. With him will be the false prophet who apparently knew everything and led the people astray. Whenever God is rejected, deception follows. We cannot reject God and remain the same. Whenever a person, a nation, or a group of people reject God, deception will follow.

Jesus will appear, and John stated that He will wage war against them. Jesus will capture the antichrist and the false prophet, and throw them alive into the fiery lake of burning sulfur. This will be easy for Jesus, and this will happen to all those who blaspheme against God. They will come to a sudden end.

Yes, God's grace is immeasurable. It is so patient, such that at times we think too patient. God is so patient that people taunt Him and say, "When will your prophecies be fulfilled? Where are all those things about which you have spoken?" They taunt God. However, there is a limit! When the line is crossed, there is sudden judgment. This will happen in personal lives, with nations and with all mankind. This is the time when God will say, "Enough!" Jesus will speak, and the people will literally become confused. We can even assume that the appearance of Jesus will cause so much confusion that people will become insane, and will turn their weapons against each other. There will be an unspeakable blood bath.

The events that will take place are nothing else but payment for sin. God had tried to keep people from this. He had placed many obstacles in their paths so that they would not follow their own ways. God granted people hundreds, even thousands of years. He gave many warnings, told them to stop, to turn around from their paths. In response, mankind made fun of God. God can do nothing but give His just punishment. It will be a tragic event, for the price of sin had already been paid by Jesus on the cross—all the people had to do was accept that gift and turn their lives around.

It will be a terrible day for those who did not know God and for all the nations of the world, but it will also be a day of God's righteousness. God's word admonishes as well as encourages us to trust Him, to follow Him and to love Him.

Psalm 2 also speaks of this day; we find in verses 1–2, 6 and 9–12:

"Why do the nations conspire and the peoples plot in vain? The kings of the earth rise up and the rulers band together against the LORD and against his anointed one…I have installed my king on Zion, my holy hill. "[He] will rule them with an iron scepter; [He] will dash them to pieces like pottery…Therefore, you kings, be wise; be warned, you rulers of the earth. Serve the Lord with fear and rejoice with trembling. Kiss the Son, lest he be angry."

In other words, get into a relationship with Jesus so that you won't be destroyed. The Psalm ends with the words, *"Blessed are all who take refuge in Him."*

No one can help us except Jesus. Only those who are in Christ are safe. May all of us have a relationship with Jesus, submit to Him and open our hearts to all that He wants to give us, so that He can fill us with his Holy Spirit. Let us remain on this path! We will be misunderstood and ridiculed by those who live in darkness. Let us warn people, telling as many as possible that they too can have salvation in Christ.

SATAN WILL
BE BOUND

REVELATION 20:1–3, 7–10

T he Bible tells us that God will settle the account with Satan after the
judgment of the antichrist, the false prophet and ungodly people.
Satan's names are mentioned in the first verses of this chapter. The
Bible calls him the dragon. This reveals his beastly and brutal nature;
the Bible also refers to him as that ancient serpent, which shows the
crafty and seductive ways he used to seduce people throughout all ages.
The Bible uses yet another name for the devil, deceiver. We must
realize one thing; in his dragon-like nature he uses his wily powers to
fulfill his aim, which is to deceive and confuse mankind. As we are well
aware, our world is in a total state of confusion! In Luke, Jesus said that
perplexity would increase greatly. This will come from the confusion
brought on by the devil. The Bible also calls him Satan. Satan means
the accuser. If those who serve God make one mistake, he accuses
them. He is also known as the accuser of the brethren.

In Revelation 20, the Bible discusses three places in the hereafter. I
think it is important to examine these. The places mentioned are the
pit, Abyss in Greek; the lake of burning sulfur, known as Gahanna or
Tophet in the Old and New Testament; and the underworld, Hades or
Scheol.

Let us examine each of these places more intensely in order to better understand what the Bible is saying. I shall begin with the underworld, with Hades. This word is usually translated as hell. It can be found sixty-five times in the Old Testament and eleven times in the New Testament. In reality, this is not the actual hell, and yet it is not incorrect to call it hell, because it is like a hell.

Jesus is the only one who can and has given us a glimpse of Hades, or the underworld. Biblical scholars know the well-known story found in Luke 16 of the rich man and poor Lazarus. Jesus describes something very interesting. There are two men, one who was very wealthy and put his trust in material things, and the poor one who had nothing and put his whole trust in God. Both had to die. We are told that angels carried Lazarus to Abraham's side. The rich man woke up in a different place. Jesus told us there are two different places in Hades. You must stay in the place where you arrive. He also mentioned there is a great chasm between the two places, and one cannot cross from one side to the other. He also tells us something about the people there. They are conscious, they can hear, they can see, they can talk, they can feel, they can taste, they have retained their memories and they have a complete understanding about the things they had heard and rejected while on earth. That is why the rich man knew that he should have repented, and that his brothers on earth should repent; otherwise they too would come to this place.

The Bible tells us that Jesus went into the underworld after His death on Golgotha. The Bible refers to the fact that until this time the devil had the key to this underworld. Ephesians 4: 8–10 and Hebrews 2:14 tell us that Jesus Christ went there and took the power of death and the key of death from the devil. He took all those who were on the righteous side and led them into Paradise. Since Jesus' death on the cross, when a righteous person dies he no longer goes to Hades, but will go to Paradise. The unrighteous will continue to go there. In 2 Corinthians 5:6–8, we read, *"Therefore we are always confident and know that as long as we are at home in the body we are away from the Lord. For we live by faith, not by sight. We are confident, I say, and would prefer to be away from the body and at home with the Lord."*

The Lord did not remain in the underworld. That is why Paul wrote in Philippians 1:23, *"I am torn between the two: I desire to depart* and be with Christ, which is better by far." He continues to say that whether we live or die, we shall be with the Lord. The righteous now go to Jesus in Paradise. The unrighteous will continue to go to the same place as before, to Hades, and will await judgment before the great white throne.

One of the other places is the Abyss. This is mentioned nine times in the New Testament, seven of which are in Revelation. In Luke 8:28 and 31, Jesus mentions this place when he meets the man from Gerasenes, who said, "What do you want with me, Jesus Son of the Most High God?...And they begged Jesus repeatedly not to order them to go into the Abyss." In Romans 10:7, we are warned not to say that Jesus comes from the Abyss, as if He was a demon. The Bible makes it very clear: the Abyss is a prison for the fallen angels and for fallen spirits. In Jude 1:6 we read, "And the angels who did not keep their positions of authority but abandoned their proper dwelling—these he has kept in darkness, bound with everlasting chains for judgment on the great Day." In the Abyss fallen angels are bound, waiting for the Day of Judgment. We read in Revelation 9 that out of the prison of the fallen angels, locusts will come forth, and during the time of the Tribulation, they will torment the people with the power of scorpions.

In Revelation 11:7, and 17:8, we read that the beast, the antichrist, will come out of the Abyss. We can interpret this to mean that the spirit which inhabits the antichrist is a demon who has been released from the Abyss and will take control of the antichrist. That is the reason for all of the horror during the Tribulation.

The Bible tells us that when the battle of Armageddon is over, the devil will be bound. He will be thrown into the place known as the Abyss, not into Hades. The prison will be locked and sealed. He will be together with his angels.

The Bible also speaks of the burning lake of sulfur; this is the actual hell. It is mentioned in the Old Testament and repeated twelve times in the New Testament. Jesus said in Matthew 5:29–30:

> "If your right eye causes you to stumble, gouge it out and throw
> it away. It is better for you to lose one part of your body than
> for your whole body to be thrown into hell. And if your right
> hand causes you to stumble, cut it off and throw it away. It is

better for you to lose one part of your body than for your whole body to go into hell."

This is the burning lake of sulfur, the Gehenna. This name was also given to the Valley of Hinnon, where the Israelites sacrificed their children to the god Moloch, during the time of their idol worship. This valley became a garbage dump during Jesus' time.

The Bible explicitly tells us that the burning lake of sulfur, the actual hell, was made for the devil and his angels. Matthew 25:41 says, *"Then he will say to those on his left, 'Depart from me, you who are cursed, into the eternal fire prepared for the devil and his angels.' Then they will go away to eternal punishment, but the righteous to eternal life."* The lake of burning sulfur was made for the devil and his angels, not for people.

Revelation tells us that the antichrist, the beast and the prophet will be thrown into this lake. In Revelation 20, we read that after being held captive for one thousand years, the devil was set free, again deceiving people, and will be thrown into this lake of burning sulfur. The Bible tells us that the beast and the false prophet were already there. They will not be destroyed. Notice, the antichrist and his prophet will be the first to be thrown into the burning lake of sulfur. One thousand years later, the devil and all the fallen angels will join them, followed sometime later by all whose names are not written in the Book of Life. Fallen angels and all people who will have to go there will first be judged. According to the universal law of God, they will deserve to go to hell.

Now can we understand why Jesus Christ came to this world? Jesus did not come just to give us a better life, or to make a more moral world. Jesus Christ came to save people from this hell. The most important thing in our life is this salvation. It is either to be lost and in hell, or to be saved and in heaven. We may be able to live a good life and have success due to our own strength and initiative; however, the main thing is not about our life on earth, but about our life after death. And this will come; it comes for everyone.

What did Jesus tell His disciples? He told them, *"Do not rejoice that the spirits submit to you, but rejoice that your names are written in heaven"* (Luke 10:20). This is the reason why we should rejoice. The

Bible tells us all whose names are not found in the Book of Life will be thrown into the lake of burning sulfur. Then it will be too late for evermore!

Do all of us who are reading these words know whether our name is written in the Book of Life? Are we certain that we are children of God? This is what matters. And thank God, we are able to know this. We need not have any doubts. Jesus Christ came to save us. The Bible tells us that he who has the Son has eternal life. Have all of us accepted Him as Lord and Savior? Do we live just for ourselves? Stubbornness, egotism, to be your own boss, and not to submit to God are all characteristics of the devil's nature. This is why Jesus said we must be born again, and we must change our attitude. Our names must be found in the Book of Life—that is what is important.

There will be a time on earth when the devil will be bound for one thousand years. During that time, Jesus will be Lord and King of this earth. He will reign from Jerusalem. At the end of these one thousand years, the devil will be freed from the Abyss. The unthinkable will happen. Many people will once again allow the devil to deceive them. Jesus will fight against him one more time and will win the battle. The antichrist, who is already in the burning lake of sulfur, will get company. The devil will be thrown into the burning lake of sulfur.

For those who are in Christ and have a relationship with Him, the devil is now already a conquered foe. Jesus offers us such security! Is each of us secure in Jesus? We may ask why Satan has to be released again. The Bible does not give us a direct answer. We can only surmise that the devil will be set free to confirm whether all people submitted to God of their own free will. The people, during the thousand years of peace, will have the opportunity to use their free will. Unfortunately, many will allow themselves to be misled, but all who choose to listen to God will be secure in Jesus Christ.

This is the reason for Jesus' coming, and why today He works on this earth—through His Word, through the Holy Spirit, through His servants, and through His church. This is why He wants us to give our lives to Him, and to follow Him in order to be saved. Let us not just look at things relative to our material and earthly lives. Let us always think of what will occur after the end time. It will definitely happen! Let us make certain that our names are written in the Book of Life!

THE FIRST AND THE SECOND RESURRECTION

REVELATION 20:4–6, 13

W e cannot find one specific passage describing everything about the resurrection. We do find that throughout the Bible many different people, who did not know each other and lived at different times, were inspired by the same Holy Spirit. They wrote from a completely different perspective about the same event. The Bible discusses the truths about the first and second resurrection in different passages. God stated that there will be a resurrection of the dead. We can read about it in Matthew 22:23–31. Jesus was in a conversation with the Sadducees, who were very intelligent people. They were certain that they had cornered Jesus, because they thought no one could argue against their logic. They said:

> "That same day the Sadducees, who say there is no resurrection, came to him with a question. 'Teacher,' they said, 'Moses told us that if a man dies without having children, his brother must marry the widow and raise up offspring for him. Now there were seven brothers among us. The first one married and died, and since he had no children, he left his wife to his brother. The same thing happened to the second and third brother, right on down to the seventh. Finally, the woman died. Now then, at the

resurrection, whose wife will she be of the seven, since all of them were married to her?' Jesus replied, 'You are in error.'"

Jesus did not mince words, but spoke clearly and directly. He did not say maybe, perhaps, or it could be that you have a wrong impression. He told them plainly, *"You are in error."* If someone is in error, he is wrong and Jesus said, *"You are in error, because you do not know the Scriptures or the power of God."* He told them there was to be a resurrection. They hung their heads in shame and left.

In Acts 26:8, we find Paul before King Agrippa. He was a prisoner, and had to defend himself because of his faith. He said the following to the king: *"Why should any of you consider it incredible that God raises the dead?"* The Bible teaches there is absolutely no doubt about a resurrection of the dead.

The second thing the Bible teaches is that there is a difference between the righteous and the unrighteous in the resurrection. God's Word says in Luke 14:14, *"Although they cannot repay you, you will be repaid at the resurrection of the righteous."* The Bible is speaking about a resurrection for the righteous. We can read similar passages in John 6:40, 44, and 54. These scriptures always discuss the resurrection of the righteous, and point out that there is a difference between the resurrection of the righteous and the resurrection of the unbelievers— those who are not saved.

The Bible clearly teaches that the lost, the unsaved, will also be resurrected. We can find this in the Old Testament. Daniel mentioned it in Daniel 12:2: *"Multitudes who sleep in the dust of the earth."* Daniel uses the phrase *"multitudes who sleep in the dust"* when he is talking of the people who have died. He said that they *"...will awake: some to everlasting life, others to shame and everlasting contempt."* Daniel already mentioned there would be a difference, and both the saved and unsaved will be resurrected.

In John 5:28– 29, Jesus said, *"Do not be amazed at this, for a time is coming when all who are in their graves will hear his voice and come out—those who have done what is good will rise to live, and those who have done what is evil will rise to be condemned."* In Acts 24:15 it says, *"...and I have the same hope in God as these men themselves have, that there will be a resurrection of both the righteous and the wicked."*

Thus, the Bible teaches that all mankind will be resurrected. It also teaches there will be a difference between the resurrection of the saved and the resurrection of the unsaved. The Bible also teaches there will be a time span of one thousand years between the resurrection of the saved and the unsaved. This is written in Revelation 20:5: *"(The rest of the dead did not come to life until the thousand years were ended.) This is the first resurrection."*

As Christians, we are probably more interested in what the Bible has to say about the resurrection of the righteous. If we are God's children, we are interested in hearing the description of the resurrection of His children. The Bible teaches that the resurrection of the righteous will not occur at the same time for all the righteous. Let us look at 1 Corinthians 15: 20–24: *"But Christ has indeed been raised from the dead,"* that is how Paul begins. This declaration leaves no room for argument. He continues:

> *"The first fruits of those who have fallen asleep. For since death came through a man, the resurrection of the dead comes also through a man. For as in Adam all die, so in Christ all will be made alive. But each in turn: Christ, the first fruits; then, when he comes, those who belong to him."*

It is interesting to note that the Holy Spirit makes a comparison of the resurrection with the Feast of the First Born, found in Leviticus 23. There we find the description of the different feasts of the Israelites. Each of these feasts has a parallel in the New Testament. One was the Feast of the First Fruits. The Feast of Thanksgiving pertains to this. First, the Israelites had to go out to their fields on the first day of a given week to harvest the first ripe grains. They were to bring this harvest to the priest, who would offer it to God. The real time of harvest would come fifty days later when the complete harvest would be brought in. Sometime later, there would be a second harvest. The Holy Spirit is using this picture when He is speaking of the resurrection of the righteous.

He said each would be resurrected according to his turn. Jesus was the first to be resurrected from the dead with a transfigured body. In the Old and New Testaments, others came back to life. They lived for a time, and then died again. Jesus was the first to be resurrected with a new body, the first fruit. As Jesus rose from the dead, we read in Matthew 27: 51–53, *"At that moment the curtain of the temple was torn in two from top to bottom. The earth shook, the rocks split and the tombs broke open. The bodies of many holy people who had died were raised to life. They came out of the tombs after Jesus' resurrection."* When did this take place? It was after Jesus' resurrection as the first one to do so. We can safely assume there was not only a harvest of the first fruits in the Old Testament church, but also there will be a harvest of the first fruits in the New Testament church.

We have discussed the Rapture and learned that not everyone will be Raptured and taken up to God at the same time. Some will have to go through the Tribulation when there will be second Rapture. The Bible tells us about this sequence. God's Word tells us that after the first fruits it will be those who belong to Him, the large multitude of believers, who will go with Him. There will be a second harvest. It will be the harvest of those who go through the Tribulation, who died, and were not ready to go with Him when he came. The last ones to be resurrected will be those who died without Christ, and who went into eternity without Him.

Not one of us can influence the reality of the resurrection. This will happen whether we like it or not! We can influence one thing, and that is the time of our resurrection. Will it be with the righteous, or with the unrighteous? We determine that ourselves. God has not predetermined this. God has left this decision to each of us personally, depending upon our acceptance of His son, Jesus Christ. We have to let this sink in over and over again. God's Word tells us it is our personal relationship with Jesus Christ which will determine whether we shall be among the righteous or the unrighteous.

Some may say, "I have nothing against Jesus. I value what He did. It really impresses me that He went to the cross and gave up His life. I have often thanked Him for this." This is not what matters. Jesus said, *"If you love me, keep my commandments."* Jesus does not want to be admired. He wants us to accept His authority over us. *"If you love me, keep my commandments."* There are some who want to be saved, others who want to be baptized, and there are people who wish to live holy lives, to obey God and to break away from sin;

however, not today, it is always tomorrow or the day after. This is the uncertainty of our lives. What would happen if we had to appear before Jesus as we are today?

THE MILLENNIUM AND THE LAST JUDGMENT

REVELATION 20:6—15

H ere we have two events: first the millennium and then the judgment before the white throne. We shall look at some of the important aspects and features of these two events.

It has always been a dream and desire of mankind to establish a kingdom of peace on this earth. History will show us that there has always been someone who had this dream. There were times when certain men believed they were close to establishing such a kingdom. The world is still calling out for peace, even in our time. But the real meaning of peace is vastly misunderstood by mankind.

No one has ever succeeded in establishing this kingdom. Yet, it will come some day! There will be a time when peace will reign on this earth. This peace will not arrive through the efforts or power of man. It will arrive when the Prince of Peace reigns! God's Word tells us that the devil will be bound for one thousand years, and will be imprisoned in the Abyss after the antichrist and the prophet have been thrown into the burning lake of sulfur. Then, the one who had deceived people by war and hatred will be gone. Jesus Christ, with the multitude of the righteous, will then return to the earth. Mankind's dream will become a reality! There will be a theocratic government; God Himself will rule this world through His Son, Jesus Christ. All those who accepted Jesus during the Dispensation of the Church, who opened their hearts and allowed Him to establish His kingdom in them, will reign with Him. The positions of authority in this new kingdom will be determined in accordance with how much we allowed Jesus to rule in our lives. If we do not give Jesus any room to reign in our hearts now, and if we want to control our own lives and follow our own wishes and desires, then the possibility exists that we may be saved, but will not reign when He establishes His kingdom.

Jerusalem will become the capital city; it becomes more and more evident that this region is being developed toward this purpose. There is hardly a day that the media does not report something about this area. At the same time, the uncertainty of how this region will continue increases.

God's Word tells us that a world government will intervene in this area. There are increasing developments. A world government was seen as a possible solution at one of the G-20 meetings. Even the Pope spoke about the necessity of a world government. The antichrist will introduce this world government. By the way, most people will not recognize him for who he is. It all has to take place: the reign of the antichrist, the development toward Jerusalem and the spotlight on the Middle East. The reign of the antichrist will be relatively short, and then Jesus will come and establish His kingdom.

God's Word tells us that during Jesus' reign there will be unprecedented global economic growth. We read about this in Amos 19: 13: "'The days are coming,' declares the LORD, 'when the reaper will be overtaken by the plowman and the planter by the one treading grapes. New wine will drip from the mountains and flow from all the hills.'" One harvest will be followed by another. We read something similar in Joel 3:18, and Isaiah 35:1 also discusses this economic growth. Many other Bible verses talk about the same event. The Bible also tells us that people will age differently during the millennium. In Isaiah 65, it is written that if a person dies at the age of one hundred, he will be like the age of a child. When the One who created man reigns on earth, and when the enemy of mankind who came to earth through sin and death is gone, there will be totally different conditions in place. The Bible tells us that the earth will be overflowing with Jesus Christ, the King, the Glory of God!

The Bible states there will be distinctive climatic changes. All of creation will be affected by the peace and by the redemption that will come over the earth. Paul wrote in Romans 8:19–23, that all of creation is waiting for that day, and in Isaiah 11: 6–8, the Bible describes something we cannot imagine. Beasts of prey will suddenly be tame, and children will play with snakes. Unimaginable changes will occur on this earth! What mankind has always longed for will be here, peace with God, peace in nature, and peace in people's relationships with each other—all of this will be here. That will be the time as is mentioned in Isaiah 2:2–5:

> "In the last days the mountain of the LORD's temple will be established as the highest of the mountains; it will be exalted above the hills, and all nations will stream to it. Many peoples will come and say, 'Come, let us go up to the mountain of the LORD, to the temple of the God of Jacob. He will teach us his ways, so that we may walk in his paths.' The law will go out from Zion, the word of the LORD from Jerusalem. He will judge between the nations and will settle disputes for many peoples. They will beat their swords into plowshares and their spears into pruning hooks. Nation will not take up sword against nation, nor will they train for war anymore. Come, descendants of Jacob, let us walk in the light of the LORD."

There is no other event in the Bible with as many prophecies given as there are about this Kingdom. This is the Kingdom which the disciples expected when Jesus was with them, and will also be the Kingdom where Jerusalem is awaiting Jesus. God's word tells us that near the end of the thousand years, the devil will be released. This will prove that education by itself does not change people. Man's heart is basically wicked, and many will turn against God after the devil is released. Each person who serves God must do so out of his own free will. The generations during this time will have the opportunity to decide for or against God. The Bible tells us this time will end with a terrible new judgment for those who reject God.

The millennium will come, and no one can prevent it. However, all of us have the opportunity to avoid the judgment, which I shall now discuss. We must be informed about this judgment because it can affect us personally. *"I saw a great white throne and him who was seated on it."* This should remind us of John's vision in Revelation 4, where he also saw a throne. Upon comparing both of these descriptions, we shall find a great difference between them. Revelation 4 discusses the throne of mercy, a throne that has a rainbow over it, a throne where one can receive forgiveness and help. In this chapter it is the throne of justice and no longer of mercy.

In connection to this, John saw the dead arise, the great and the small. These are the ones about whom it said in Revelation 20:5, *"The rest of the dead did not come to life until the thousand years were ended."* We have already discussed the two resurrections—the resurrection of the righteous, which occurred about one thousand years before the resurrection of the unrighteous. At this point, all of the righteous have been resurrected. John saw the great and the small, the distinguished people who made a name for themselves, the popular people, people who had some influence on earth, people who had power, and also those who were unimportant. He saw all of them come back to life, all of them unrighteous. He saw how the seas gave up the dead, those who had drowned, and he saw the dead come out of Hades.

While he was seeing these resurrected dead, he noticed something interesting and wrote it down. He said that books were opened, and the Book of Life was opened. These are not all the same books. The people will be judged. These books are the ones in which God has kept His accounts. We have to realize that God takes note of everything we do. The day will come when the books will be opened, and the Bible states very clearly that people will be judged according to their deeds. This judgment will not take into account whether one is saved or not. All those appearing at this judgment are *lost!*

Just as a Christian receives a reward or will experience loss according to his deeds, so will the people who had rejected Christ be judged according to their deeds. Let us not forget: God is a just God. He will also treat the unrighteous fairly. Not everyone will receive the same punishment. The sentence will be according to their deeds. However, *all* whose names are not written in the Book of Life shall be thrown into the burning lake of sulfur. This will be horrible. Even there, there will be different degrees of punishment. It cannot be expressed more clearly: God takes notes!

Why are Christians not afraid of this judgment? At the very moment when a person accepts Jesus Christ as his Lord and Savior and Jesus takes residence in his heart and his sins are forgiven, his ledger of guilt will be torn up. Everything negative about his life will be deleted. His name will be entered into the Book of Life! This is my only hope to be able to stand before God, that the blood of Jesus has covered all of my sins. The judgment will come according to what is written in the book. The Book of Life will be opened to prove that their names are not written there. They will go to the place where God will send the people who have rejected Christ.

Now we can understand why Jesus told His disciples, on returning from one of their missions filled with joy, that they should not rejoice because the evil spirits submitted to them, and that they had experienced their deliverance; instead, they should rejoice that their names were written in the Book of Life. There is nothing more important or vital for us than the realization that our name is written in the Book of Life! Our health, our prosperity and the length of our life are all secondary to the importance of having our name written in the Book of Life.

We are able to know whether our name is written in the Book of Life—we have to know! The Bible says that the Spirit of God gives our spirit the confirmation that we are children of God. I do not desire anything more than to have this inner confirmation. *"If anyone's name was not found written in the Book of Life, he was thrown into the lake of fire,"* to the place where the antichrist, the false prophet and devil are. How long will people remain in this place? They will remain there just as long as people will remain in heaven. The Bible says forever and ever. The same words which are used for the redeemed—that they will remain with God forever—are also used for the lost. They will remain in the burning lake forever. There is no other expression. I shall repeat it one more time as clearly as I can: the reason Jesus came to this earth is to save mankind—us—from this lake of fire.

There is nothing more urgent for a person than salvation. I would like to caution you about messages: ones that only uphold rituals, that only teach how to get along with your fellow man, or that only indoctrinate a social gospel, and that do not teach the true gospel message of the Bible. The Bible's message is that man is lost, and because he has a sinful nature he must be saved, and there is only one possible way—salvation through Jesus Christ!

We can strive to be a good person, and we may succeed. What is important is whether our sins have been forgiven through the blood of Jesus, whether our names are written in the Book of Life, and whether we are born again. There is only one way to be saved. May the Holy Spirit reveal this truth to each of us so that we would humble ourselves before God and declare, "Lord I am willing to accept your Word, to submit to your Word, and to change my human opinions because I want to be saved, and to have the assurance that I am born again."

The millennium will come, and the throne will be erected. All those who have not accepted Jesus Christ as their Lord and Savior will have to appear before the white throne. Today, God is still speaking to us. We do not have to be a part of that group. We can be part of the Resurrection of the redeemed, which has different criteria. We shall be in heaven where we shall receive our rewards from Jesus Christ, and then we shall reign with Him and be His servants. Now it is our responsibility to call people to come to Jesus Christ, and those who allow themselves to be called shall be saved.

A NEW HEAVEN
AND A NEW EARTH

"I saw a new heaven and a new earth."

This is the last major event in the Bible. The fall of man not only corrupted himself, but also all of God's creation. The Bible tells us when God created the earth and all there was therein, He looked at it, and all of it was good. We can rest assured that if God said that it was good, then it was good. Since the fall of man, things on earth have not been so good. Let us begin with man.

Man's disobedience and his rebellion have caused the separation of an intimate relationship with our creator, God. Instead of creatively working together with God, man got further and further away from Him, and put himself in the center of things. Due to this situation—the separation from God—man's body became subjected to sickness and sorrow. We must not say that a person's sin has caused his sickness. Sickness is a result of the fall of man. Not only was man's relationship with God destroyed and his body affected, but all of creation, which had been put under the jurisdiction of man, has also suffered. Paul wrote that all creation is longing and waiting for the revelation of the Son of God.

After the fall, and once things started to deteriorate, there was no other choice for God but to begin again. Jesus Christ was the start of something new. God had to start at the root of the problem. First, he had to renew man's heart through Jesus Christ. The root of all evil, the root of wickedness, is inside the heart of man. The Bible says that God will not only change our hearts and through Jesus give us new hearts, but our body will be changed at the time of the resurrection of the dead. Thank God, children of God are able to experience some of the power of the resurrection because our bodies can already receive strength and healing.

The Bible says that at the end, God will create a new heaven and a new earth. Someone may ask, "What is this heaven?" That the earth is in need of a renewal is quite obvious. However, is the heaven in which God resides not well enough? I believe that it is very good. The Bible talks about three heavens. There is the heaven where the birds of the air fly. There is the heaven where the planets and suns are, and there is the heaven where God is. No satellite has ever reached the latter.

The Bible mentions the three heavens. I do not believe when the Bible speaks of a new heaven and a new earth that it speaks of the universe, the starry sky or the heaven in which God lives, but it speaks of our earth, and the sky which surrounds the earth. The Bible speaks about this. In Isaiah 65:17, we can find this prophecy. We are actually called upon to wait for a new heaven. *"See, I will create new heavens and a new earth. The former things will not be remembered, nor will they come to mind."*

The new heaven and the new earth will not be comparable to our present ones. The new earth will be so beautiful that we shall not think of the old one. Can we understand why Jesus tells us not to be so attached to this earth? Do we really comprehend this? Everything will pass away; it has no lasting value. However, whatever the Lord does in us, and whatever we do out of sincere and pure motives, will have eternal value. When will this earth be renewed? When will a new heaven and a new earth be created? It may be during the Judgment at the great white throne during the final judgment of the unrighteous. Peter, in 2 Peter 3:7, speaks about a fire that will destroy all ungodly men. Perhaps this same fire will renew, purify and cleanse heaven and earth. However it may be, God will do it. The new heaven and the new earth will become the home for the redeemed. We shall now discuss this new home.

It is difficult to find words to describe the beauty of this new home. The Holy Spirit mentions mainly things that will not be there, but does help us to visualize how it will be. We get, at least to some degree, a wonderful picture of the beauty of this place. The Bible says there will be no pain. Isn't this fabulous? All of us have experienced pain—some more, some less—and we know how awful pain can be. There is physical pain which hurts and causes exhaustion. There is also psychological pain which is terrible and devastating. Those who work in hospitals know that whether the pain is physical or psychological, it is real. In heaven there will be no more pain!

God's word also says there will be no more sorrow. This is not the same as pain. The fact is some people are being tested. This is not because they are worse than others. There are just some people who seem to be going through times of testing. What times of sorrow can come over some families and some nations! The Bible says there will be neither pain nor sorrow.

Furthermore, the Bible says there will be no more troubles. That will be fantastic! It is so easy to say, "Do not worry." We all worry too much! The more we get to know God and the more intimate our relationship is with Him, the closer we come to worrying less. I am not saying that we will achieve the ultimate, but the closer we live with God, the more we allow God's Spirit to guide our lives, and the more He can change our attitudes, the closer we arrive at the goal. This is why Jesus tells us that we should not worry, but should throw all our cares on Him. We should learn to cast all our cares and burdens on Him; He will take care of us. In heaven there will be no more troubles or cares.

The Bible also says there will be no temptations in heaven. One problem each Christian has to face is temptation. There is temptation of the flesh, of the world, and of the devil. All of us are prone to these temptations; no one is exempt. As soon as the Holy Spirit succeeds in teaching us a new Biblical truth, the devil is right there with enormous temptation. We must fight against it. We often ask, "When will things be different?" As long as we are alive, things will not change, but the day will come when there will be no more temptations. Remember, to be tempted is not a sin. Some Christians become very depressed when they come face to face with temptation and wonder, "How can this still happen in my life?" Temptation is not a sin but it is dangerous, and requires resistance.

The Bible also says there will be no seas in heaven. Seas represent storms, unrest and separation, and God's word tells us that none of these will in heaven.

Lastly, the Bible says there will be no more death in heaven. Death, the worst of man's enemies, will be no more!

God was describing the new earth and heaven to us. He used some examples which we would understand and told us what would no longer exist there. I honestly do not believe we can actually comprehend what it will look like!

A mother gave birth to a boy who came blind into this world. When the boy was a few years old, a doctor decided to try an operation in order to give the boy some sight. The surgery was successful. When this boy finally was able to go outside and saw the beauty of nature all around him, he turned to his mother and said, "Mummy, why have you never told me how beautiful everything is?" It was impossible to do so. Try to explain color to a blind person! Try to explain a blue sky or describe a sunset to someone who cannot see. Try to explain the gorgeous colors of flowers or butterflies to someone who has never been able to see—it is impossible. It is just as difficult, and even more so, for us to imagine the beauty of the home of the redeemed. What did Paul say when he was Raptured to the third heaven? He heard words which were impossible to explain or translate into human language. He saw things which were simply unexplainable, things which God has prepared for those who love Him—The Home of the Redeemed. It is no wonder a songwriter wrote, "Heaven is a wonderful place."

God's Invitation to Everyone

Revelation 21:6-7, the Bible says, *"To him who is thirsty I will give to drink without cost from the spring of the water of life."*

This is an invitation from God. It is His wish that every person would come to this place. This is why Jesus came to this earth, this is why He died on the cross, and this is why He is working through the

Holy Spirit even today. God is looking for the thirsty. Who is thirsty? Everyone on this earth is thirsty. There is absolutely not one person who has never been thirsty. Why does a person seek pleasure? Why does a person seek anything? It is because he is thirsty. Since he is spiritually blind, he can only see what is right in front of him, and he reaches out for it, but then realizes that his heart is not filled with fresh water, and that he has become bound and enslaved.

A person can arrive at a point where he thinks that there is nothing other than what he can see, feel or touch. Therefore he says, "Eat, drink and be merry, for tomorrow you die." Then everything will be over. That is why he lives only for things of this world. When God speaks to him, he becomes arrogant and refuses to admit there is a God above who knows more than he does. This God invites us and calls out to the thirsty to come, and they will receive living water without cost. Jesus put it into these words: *"Everyone who drinks of this water will be thirsty again, but whoever drinks the water I give them will never thirst. Indeed, the water I give them will become in them a spring of water welling up to eternal life"* (John 4, 12 and 14). God invites us to come to Him to have our thirst quenched, to belong to Him and be saved. One thing is evident: an invitation is only of benefit if there is a response. We may receive an invitation to a most prestigious occasion, however, it is useless if we do not accept it. God's invitation must be accepted. This is God's desire and this is why He calls us.

He wants us to be in the home He has prepared for us. Jesus said in John 14:2– 3:

> *"In my Father's house are many rooms; if it were not so, I would have told you. I am going there to prepare a place for you. And if I go and prepare a place for you, I will come back and take you to be with me that you also may be where I am."*

It is the wish of God for man to live in this home for the redeemed. To do so, man has to be saved and filled with the water of eternal life. In this world, Christians are living in expectation of this new home. People will always accuse Christians of comforting themselves with the idea of 'later.' The Bible says that the best will come at the end. It also tells us we can have an anchor and help in this life, and that everyone who lives with God will agree. We will always be accused of being dreamers about the future, but we shall not lose our hope and joy.

In 2 Peter 3:13, Peter says, *"But in keeping with his promise we are looking forward to a new heaven and a new earth, where righteousness dwells."* There will be no unrighteousness there. Isn't that wonderful! Isn't that powerful! Wherever we look in this world we find unrighteousness, and we cannot get rid of it. In the home of the redeemed there will be no unrighteousness. Righteousness will reign there. Peter continues to say in verse 14, *"So then, dear friends, since you are looking forward to this, make every effort to be found spotless, blameless and at peace with him."* Since this is the truth, we shall not become tired nor give up, but will remain strong in our faith in Jesus Christ. We may not like everything in our lives. That is true. Let us not become tired, but let us cling to our faith.

In Hebrews 11, we read about many heroes of the faith. It always says that by faith they held fast, without seeing. Some held on by faith without experiencing it in their lifetime. They continued on by faith, and their faith will be rewarded in the Home of the Redeemed. We have many wishes in our lifetime, but we do not get everything we desire. We cannot explain everything, but there is one thing of which I am certain and the Bible tells us so: faith is never useless. This is why we shall persevere. God's word says this is true, and we shall continue to follow Him in total submission. We want to be spotless, without fault, and to live in peace. A beautiful home is waiting for each child of God. If you are not yet His, why wait?

God gives us the opportunity to work along with Him, to extend His invitation to many people. *"Come, those who are thirsty and whoever comes shall drink!"* I believe that we shall have the same experience as that little boy who was blind. When we get to be with Jesus and see what He has prepared for us, we shall say, "Lord, why did you not tell us how wonderful it is?" We are so limited! Paul wrote in 1 Corinthians 2:9, *"What no eye has seen, what no ear has heard, and what no human mind has conceived—the things God has prepared for those who love him."* This will be the proof that everything was worthwhile. We shall continue to serve and obey God, trusting in His word. We want to honor, praise and worship Him.

THE NEW JERUSALEM

REVELATION 21:9–27, 22:1–5

T hose whose names are written in the Book of Life will be the ones who are allowed to enter into this city. These are the wise virgins from Matthew 25. The Bible tells us that this city will come from God, right out of heaven.

There are many beautiful and wonderfully located cities in this world. Some people prefer older cities and their architecture, some prefer the modern ones. So much variety can be observed in this world. However, no one has ever seen anything compared to this city. There has not yet been an architect who came up with a plan to build a city, not just according to its surface measurements, but also according to its height. No one has ever accomplished such a structure, and it is even difficult to imagine this.

When Jesus left this earth, He informed His followers that He would do two things for them when He was with His Father. First of all, He would be our advocate. We can rejoice that He defends each one of us to His Father, and that we can come to the Father through Him. He is our mediator! We do not require a person, a priest, a pastor, or an elder to come to God.

Secondly, He is building something for us and is making preparations. What is He preparing? He is building a city, a home for each of us. Jesus is designing and building a city for His people. John saw this city at the conclusion of his vision, built by God, coming down from heaven unto this earth; the city which has been built for all whose names are written in the Book of Life.

In this city will be people who never owned a home while they lived on earth; they had always rented. There they will have a home built by God. John describes this city to the best of his ability. He told us its dimensions: twelve thousand stadia wide, long and high, i.e. twenty-five hundred kilometers wide, long and high. Can you imagine a city with such dimensions? Many people will be able to live there, and this will be necessary, for I believe many children of God will be there. The wall around it will be seventy-five meters wide. The foundation will be made of precious stones—imagine the array of colors! Some people believe that God is boring! God loves colors; did you know that? Just look at nature. Observe the rising and the setting of the sun. Is there anything more beautiful than all of the colors? Why are there so many colors? They are for us! They have no other purpose other than to make us happy. Picture the walls, the foundation made out of precious stones—all giving off colors—and the twelve gates of this city, each made from one pearl. As John entered this city, he looked around; he had never seen anything like it, gold that looked like glass. That must have been some purification process! I do not think that we on earth have the knowledge to perform such refinement. It will be wonderful!

He saw the outside of the city and was overwhelmed with its magnificence and beauty. He was somewhat able to describe these things. When he entered the city, he noticed that the streets were made of gold; they looked like transparent glass; he had never seen anything like this before. This was the end of the description of the inner city. John did say that there was no temple in this city. Notice what is important to John? He was a true Christian! John did not care how the individual houses and residences were constructed; he tried to locate the temple. His desire was to serve God and he could not find a temple. Then he understood—God Himself was there, a temple was not necessary!

He discovered something else. This city did not require a sun or a moon. The new earth and the new heaven did not have a sun or a moon, because there was the glory of God and the Lamb. He saw that the river of the water of life was flowing from the throne of God, and trees were planted on the banks of this river. These will be very remarkable trees; they will bear new fruit every month. This is what we shall eat. Did you ever think about this? Jesus definitely ate after His resurrection. We cannot imagine how all of this will happen, but it will, and it will taste good.

John tells us more. We shall see His face; we shall see how He looks. As long as John stood outside the city, he was occupied with the material aspect of it. Once inside, his only concern was about the One who had died for him. Do you know Jesus? Have you accepted Him as your personal Lord and Savior? Do you serve Him by faith, without seeing Him? Do you serve Him as if He were here? There will be a new heaven, a new earth and a new gorgeous city. There is a song written about this New Jerusalem. It describes Jerusalem during the time of Jesus, at the time of the crucifixion, and continues with the writer's imagination of how the New Jerusalem will look, the city that will last forever, the city which God has prepared for those who serve and love Him. Will you be there?

The

REMNANT

RESTORING INTEGRITY
to AMERICAN
MINISTRY

Holy Bible

LARRY
STOCKSTILL

Restoring the Call to Personal Integrity
Order at:

//remnant.bethany.com